Money

Anxiety

How Financial Uncertainty Changes

Consumer Behavior And The Economy

First Edition Design Publishing

Money Anxiety
Copyright ©2013 Dan Geller
ISBN 978-1622-874-76-7 PRINT
ISBN 978-1622-874-77-4 EBOOK

LCCN 2013956364

December 2013

Published and Distributed by
First Edition Design Publishing, Inc.
P.O. Box 20217, Sarasota, FL 34276-3217
www.firsteditiondesignpublishing.com

Cover Art by First Edition Design Publishing
Deborah E Gordon

*In memory of my parents, Benjamin and Ester Geller,
who instilled in me the pursuit of knowledge.*

Dedication

I dedicate this book to my two daughters, Tina Geller and Moriah Geller, who bring much joy to my life, and who taught me more than I taught them; and to my family and friends who never stopped believing in me. I also dedicate this book to the many teachers, mentors and friends I had the privilege of meeting throughout the years. Specifically, I would like to mention the late Peter Goldman, who taught me more about business and human behavior than anything I found in text books; Dr. Nahum Biger, the Chairman of my dissertation committee, whose knowledge and analytical capabilities were an inspiration to me; Dr. Greg Schmid; and the late Dr. Eugene Muscat, who guided me through the maze of research, analytics and critical thinking.

Table of Contents

Preface

Often people ask me, "What do you do?" I typically pause for a second and respond, "I think." "Yes," they reply, "we all think, but what do you do for a living? Are you an economist? A psychologist?" "No," I respond, "I am neither of those—I am a thinker." The expression on peoples' faces is always the same: puzzlement. And then they usually ask, "You think? What does that mean?" "Well," I say, "I think about why things are the way they are, especially when it comes to economics and the role people play in shaping the economy."

I believe that if we had a better understanding of behavioral economics, we would be able to smooth out the drastic ups and downs of any economic cycle and thus reduce the amount of human and financial damage that comes with each major recession. That's what I think about, and that is what started the long journey of research, exploration and understanding that I am going to share with you in this book.

My exploratory journey into behavioral economics started because I wanted to know why we experience ups and down in the economy, and how we can use greater insight in planning for the future. My quest for better understanding of the economy was not from a conventional economics perspective such as the makeup of Gross Domestic Product (GDP) or many other indicators economists use to measure the economy. Rather, I wanted to understand the underlying reason—the human behavior element behind the economic indicators, and how it impacts the economy.

My quest for better understanding of the economy started in the mid-2000s, when the U.S. economy was at its peak. Housing prices were sky high and consumers were spending money like there was no tomorrow. "What is it," I asked myself, "that makes the economy forge forward so forcefully and rapidly?" Being a non-economist freed me to view this phenomenon from a neutral prospective rather than the traditional "supply and demand" view. I started looking for other reasons that explain the motivation people have to spend more and save less during certain times, and to reverse course during times of economic recession.

As a trained researcher and analyst, I was able to look at data objectively and isolate myself from various commentaries and interpretations of events. I was able to look strictly at empirical data about consumer financial behavior rather than consider what consumers said about their behavior. This approach led me to uncover one of the main new concepts in behavioral economics, which I will discuss in length later in this book—the gap between what consumers say and what they actually do. I named this gap "the confidence gap". It explains why sometimes there is a difference between traditional reading of consumer confidence and their actual financial behavior. Observing the confidence gap made me even more determined to find an empirical method to demonstrate the difference between what consumers say and what they actually do. The main challenge in measuring financial anxiety objectively, rather than recording what consumers say subjectively, is that financial confidence or anxiety is a factor—not an indicator. In statistics, we distinguish between variables that can be observed and measured—such as the amount of money consumers spend every month—and factors, which are latent variables and cannot be observed or measured directly. A classic example of a latent variable is financial fear and anxiety. As you will see later in the book, after years of experimentation, I was able to use a special statistical model called Structural Equation Modeling (SEM) to measure the impact consumer financial anxiety has on two critical components of the economy—savings and spending.

Once the statistical model for measuring consumer financial anxiety was developed, I tested it going back 50 years, and lo and behold, it perfectly explains the various economic ups and downs of the last half century. Moreover, the model was very accurate in predicting the last recession of 2007-2009 even before other consumer confidence indices did so. I name the newly developed statistical model for measuring financial anxiety "Money Anxiety Index", and I will discuss this index in detail later in the book.

The ability to measure the level of consumer financial anxiety though the Money Anxiety Index opened the door to many other observations that will change the way we measure the real impact consumer financial anxiety has on the economy. Moreover, I will demonstrate later in the book the fallacy of conventional price elasticity of demand for retail goods and services as well as yields on financial services. I will demonstrate why the conventional price elasticity model should be modified to account for the level of consumer financial anxiety.

Another area that will greatly benefit from the ability to measure financial anxiety is consumer segmentation. Currently, the only two main segmentation methods are demographics, which groups consumers according to their age, income range, gender, education and the like. The other segmentation method is typology or psychographics, which segments consumers based on their "type", such as Innovators, Achievers and the like. The focal point of this book is the introduction of a new method of segmentation—Behavioralogy, which segments actual behavior. I am going to refer to behavioralogy as an orientation model because behavioralogy does not actually segment consumers into defined types or groups, but rather it identifies the orientation consumers have towards various economic conditions. The importance of behavioralogy is that it provides insight into how consumers behave regardless of their demographic or psychographic classification. As you will, consumers react similarly to varying economic conditions regardless of their demographic or psychographic classification.

The behavioralogy orientation matrix is a game changer because it is highly predictable, due to the fact that it is based on objective human behavior rather than on subjective statements about behavior. Human behavior never changes—only circumstances do. Thus, analysts, economists, practitioners and business people can anticipate the impact on the economy as a whole, or on their specific field, when the level of consumer financial anxiety rises or falls. I have verified the applicability of the behavioralogy matrix over decades of data and during varying economic conditions, and it worked without fail.

So after many years of rigorous research and analysis, trial and error, frustration and elation, I finally put it all together in this book so you can benefit from this added knowledge and understanding of the link between human financial behavior and the economy. I know of no segment of the economy that cannot benefit from the application of behavioralogy, and I am confident that many of you will put this knowledge to good use. Moreover, I hope that the application of behavioralogy will positively impact peoples' financial standing by providing them with greater insight into what to expect in each stage of an economic cycle and how to protect themselves against major and sudden losses.

Introduction

Our ancestors hoarded food and wood to protect themselves from life-threatening dangers such as the elements and predatory animals. We don't face the same dangers today, but our instinctive behavior remains the same when we face financial danger due to economic uncertainty.

This is a behavioral economics book showing readers how money anxiety impacts consumer financial behavior and the economy. Readers will see how a high level of money anxiety changes consumers' saving and spending behavior, and the impact this change has on retail sales and bank savings. This knowledge will allow business and financial people to reduce expenses during times of high money anxiety, and increase revenues during times of low money anxiety.

The book describes the results of my research showing how the level of money anxiety leads to six types of consumer financial behaviors. The six behavioral types, referred to as Behavioralogy, were developed based on scientific research into the connection between consumer financial anxiety and the economy. These findings show that the state of the economy is inversely correlated to consumers' level of money anxiety. When the level of money anxiety is up, the economy is down; and when money anxiety is down, the economy is up.

The book shows how consumers change their saving and spending patterns based on their level of money anxiety, and how this in turn impacts the economy. When money anxiety increases, consumers save more and spend less, which pushes the economy into a recession. Conversely, when money anxiety decreases, consumers save less and spend more, which expands the economy.

Economics is a complex subject even for economists—just try to get ten economists to reach a consensus on the current state of the economy. This book simplifies economic assessment by showing readers how the money anxiety level changes consumers' financial behavior and how this impacts the economy, without the need to study and review dozens of complex economic indicators and projection models.

This book allows readers to be proactive and take preventive measures in anticipation of changes in consumers' money anxiety and their financial behavior. When the level of money anxiety is trending upwards, retail business should adjust pricing and inventories to the "Durable Diet" type of behavioralogy, and banks should gear up for the "Mattress Money" type of financial behavior.

An economy is cyclical by nature because no economy can expand or contract forever. Thus, the ability to detect shifts in the economic cycle and take proactive steps to ensure financial stability is highly desirable for business and financial people. This book provides an actual example of how the Money Anxiety Index detected the beginning of the downturn in the economy 15 months prior to the official declaration of a recession in December 2007.

This book is based on scientific research and empirical analysis from the fields of neurology, psychology, and behavioral economics. The book references research conducted by Daniel Kahneman, Ph.D., Nobel Prize recipient in economics, on thinking fast and slow; Dan Ariely, Ph.D. on irrational behavior; George Akerlof, Ph.D. and Robert Shiller, Ph.D. on behavioral economics; Deepak Chopra, M.D. and Rudolph E. Tanzi, Ph.D. on the three major components of the human brain; Leonard Mlodinow, Ph.D. on the structure and function of the brain and Nassim Nicholas Taleb, Ph.D. on the impact of the highly improbable.

The state of the local and global economy is a central theme of most news programs today and is likely to stay this way for the foreseeable future. Reports on the debt, deficit, taxation, unemployment, and housing and consumer confidence are discussed daily, and for a good reason—the last recession, a.k.a the Great Recession, had the greatest economic impact on the U.S. economy since the Great Depression.

Nearly every household in the U.S. was and is adversely impacted by the Great Recession and its aftermath, either by a job loss, declining home equity and/or diminishing investments. Most people are puzzled by the severity of the Great Recession, and all the "explanations" about derivative financial products, CDs and the like are just adding to the confusion.

People are puzzled by the sluggish economic recovery despite trillions of dollars in governmental spending and Fed stimulus. They want a simple and valid explanation of what is holding the economy back and why. This book will provide readers with a simple, empirical and logical explanation of the root cause of the sluggish economy, and how those who are involved in business or finance can leverage this knowledge to improve their business performance.

This book demonstrates how the level of financial anxiety is the main driver of the economy, and can make the difference between recession and growth. Moreover, this book makes the case that current methods of evaluating consumer confidence and calculating price elasticity are inadequate because they do not factor in the level of consumer financial anxiety.

No need to look up "behavioralogy" in the dictionary; it's not there (yet). I had to coin this term in order to describe the science of financial behavior. Behavioralogy is a combined discipline of physiology, psychology and economics—all fitting together into one scientific model that can be empirically measured and repeated. The closest discipline to behavioralogy is behavioral economics, which explains how human behavior impacts the economy. However, behavioralogy takes behavioral economics one step farther by introducing a matrix of six types of financial behavior we all share.

This is a timeless book because it deals with a timeless subject—human behavior. Human behavior never changes. The only changes throughout the ages are the circumstances humankind faces. The human reaction to varying circumstances has not changed because our reactions are built into our brain structure. This book draws on the latest research in behavioral economics, psychology and brain neurology, which together explain why we behave the way we do under varying economic conditions.

I found it very helpful to be a non-economist because I was able to have an unbiased and broader perspective on the economy. Unlike economists, who view economics through the lenses of whichever economic theory they endorse, I was able to look at events from a neutral perspective, which also includes psychology and human behavior. The advantage of this approach is that the principle presented in this book is valid regardless of an economic theory. Whether Keynesian or invisible hand, the principles of behavioralogy are valid and applicable—a rare occurrence in economics.

What's ahead in this book?

This book is divided into three logical parts, which build upon each other. In part one—Human behavior is forever—I lay the scientific foundation for financial behavior, referencing research conducted by Deepak Chopra, M.D. and Rudolph E. Tanzi, Ph.D. on the origin and functions of the three main parts of the human brain. This part of the book demonstrates the link between advanced neurological research and the latest research in psychology and behavioral economics conducted by Daniel Kahneman, Nobel Prize winner and the author of the best seller *Thinking Fast and Slow*.

In the second part of this book—Behavioralogy, the science of financial behavior—I present the six types of financial behavior (Behavioralogy) stemming from our physiological and psychological makeup. I provide empirical evidence of the impact each of the financial behavior types has on the economy, drawing from governmental sources such as the FDIC, the Fed, the U.S. Department of Commerce and the like.

And in the third part of this book—Behavioralogy in business and finance—I demonstrate the practical aspect of behavioralogy and how it can be used to measure the real price elasticity of demand of products and services. Additionally, I introduce a new model for reducing the risk associated with financial decisions. This part of the book is most helpful to business and financial people because it provides simple and practical solutions to decision that can be very costly if the wrong choice is selected. Finally, I show how the level of consumer financial anxiety is a predictor of presidential re-elections based on a perfect predictability record in the past 50 years.

Part One

Human Behavior is Forever

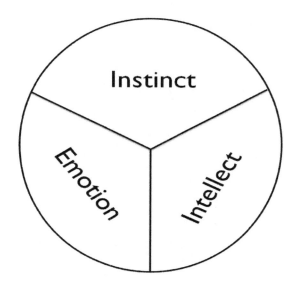

*Human behavior has not changed since Day One;
the only change was the circumstances we react to.*

Chapter One

Physiology, Psychology and Behavioralogy

Humans are creatures of habit, and for a good reason—we were "programmed" to be so as a means of survival. Survival is the strongest and most permanent feature of our being, linking our physiological, psychological and behavioral elements into a survival "machine". Throughout our evolution, we have encountered experiences that shaped our physiology, and in this case, our brain neurology. This means that the way our ancestors reacted to the danger of facing a tiger is the same reaction we use today when we face financial and economic danger. As a matter of fact, the same brain function that enacted the fight-or-flight reaction when our ancestors faced a tiger is responsible for producing our reactions to varying economic and financial conditions. Of course, the dangers of the past, which were immediate and fatal, are different from today's economics dangers, but the function of the brain that is responsible for protecting our survival does not know the difference.

During my many years of researching the topic of financial behavior I could clearly see empirical evidence of the existence of financial anxiety. I could clearly see from my analysis how the behavior and financial decisions of consumers change with varying economic conditions, but the missing part was: why? In other words, I knew that financial anxiety exists and I could see its impact empirically, but I was missing the scientific reasons for such behavior. The answers came gradually, by reading research and books by some of the leaders in the field of behavioral economics, psychology and neuroscience. I will refer to their work throughout this book to substantiate the concepts I am presenting on behavioralogy and its impact on the economy.

What is financial behavior? I would argue that it is not a stand-alone function of humans operating in a vacuum, but is the result of a specific process. In this chapter we are going to look at the process that leads to financial behavior, and the reasons we make different financial decisions according to varying economic conditions. The starting point of financial behavior, and for that matter any behavior, is our physiology or more precisely, our brain structure. Any decision we make that leads to behavior stems from our brain. Yes, even our most instinctive behavior, which we tend to think of as "gut reaction", actually originates in the brain. Once a neurological process takes place in the brain, or in some part of it as we will soon see, the process of our psychological and behavioral mode acts like a chain reaction.

Instinct, Emotion and Intellect

Let's step back and take a general look at how our brain functions in relation to decision-making and behavior. Clearly, the scope of this book is not neuroscience, but it is important to understand the role each of the three main parts of the brain plays in our decision-making process and ultimately our behavior. I found an excellent and clear description of the three main brain parts and their functions in the work of Deepak Chopra, M.D. and Rudolph E. Tanzi, Ph.D. in their latest book *Super Brain*. According to Chopra and Tanzi, the human brain has three main parts: the reptilian brain, the limbic system and the neocortex. Each of the three main parts of the human brain was formed during different times in our evolution and each part is responsible for different human functions, and therefore, behavior. In their book *Super Brain*, Chopra and Tanzi describe the functionality of each of the three brain parts as follows: "In the triune (three-part) model of the brain, the oldest part is the reptilian brain, or brain stem, designed for survival. It houses vital control centers for breathing, swallowing, and heartbeat, among other things. It also prompts hunger, sex, and the fight- or-flight response." As we will see in the proceeding chapters, the reptilian part of the brain is the origin of our instinctive behavior when we respond to real or perceived financial danger. For simplicity and clarity, I will refer to the reptilian brain as the instinctive brain.

The second main part of the brain is the limbic system, which was next to evolve. According to Chopra and Tanzi, "it houses the emotional brain and short-term memory. Emotions based on fear and desire evolved to serve the instinctive drives of the reptilian brain." Here, again, we will see later how our emotions stemming from the limbic system, affect our behavior during various times of financial uncertainty. I will refer to the limbic system part of the brain as the emotional brain.

And finally, the third main part of our brain, and our most recent addition to the brain, is the neocortex, which according to Chopra and Tanzi "is the region for intellect, decision making, and higher reasoning. As our reptilian and limbic brains drive us to do what we need to do to survive, the neocortex represents the intelligence to achieve our goals while also placing restraints on our emotions and instinctive impulses." Clearly, the neocortex is what distinguishes humans from other species because it provides us with the intellectual capacity to reason, and it acts as a balancing agent to our instinctive or emotional reaction to financial situations. I will refer to the neocortex function of the brain as the intellectual brain.

In Chopra and Tanzi's description of the three functions of the brain, I am stressing the key words that explain the link between each particular function of the brain and our financial behavior. For example, our instinctive fight-or-flight response originates in the reptilian part; our emotional response originates in our limbic system and our intellect comes from our neocortex function of the brain. A very important aspect of this brain research is the role that our intellectual function of the brain plays in "balancing" the tendency of our instinctive or emotional brain functions when reacting implosively or emotionally to economic conditions. Yet, as we will see later, in many cases our instinctive and/or emotional functions get the upper hand in the fight for control over decisions on financial matters.

Fast and Slow Thinking

The connection between our brain physiology and our heuristic process is key to our understanding of financial behavior. Heuristic is a process of decision making based on our past experiences, which is also the source of our intuition. Heuristic methods are used to speed up the process of finding solutions through mental shortcuts to ease the cognitive load of making a decision. Examples of the heuristic process include using a rule of thumb or an educated guess. We now know that each of the three main functions of our brain, instinctive, emotional and intellectual, is responsible for initiating a decision process: shall I do A, B or maybe C? This decision process, or as we will see soon decision science, is fascinating because it explains so many of our daily decisions in financial matters as well as in life in general.

The most enlightening and insightful work on heuristics and decision science originated with Amos Tversky and Daniel Kahneman in various research papers and scientific articles on this subject. Daniel Kahneman, who is a psychologist by training, is the recipient of the 2002 Nobel Prize in economics, which he would have shared with Amos Tversky, had Tversky not passed away in 1996.

In his latest book, *Thinking Fast and Slow*, Kahneman expands on the research originated by the psychologists Keith Stanovich and Richard West regarding the two modes of thinking: System 1 and System 2. According to Kahneman, "System 1 operates automatically and quickly, with no effort and no sense of voluntary control, and System 2 allocates attention to the effortful mental activities that demand it, including complex computations."

Sound familiar? Of course it does; we can clearly see the connection between our brain parts and functionality and the heuristic process that goes on in our mind when making decisions. When we look at the key attributes of our instinctive and emotional functions of the brain, they correspond with the automatic and fast decision process of System 1, and when we look at the attributes of our intellectual function of the brain, it corresponds with the mental activity, which is at the heart of System 2.

Now we have a connection between the first two of the three elements leading to financial behavior: physiology, psychology and behavioralogy. The connection between our brain function and heuristic processes is important because it supports one of the basic assertions of this book, which is that our financial decisions are explainable and therefore predictable. In other words, regardless of our financial behavior, there is a reason why we acted in one way or another, and it was not a random behavior that can't be traced or anticipated. The fact that there is a connection between our brain functionality and our decision process is the basis for behavioralogy.

The research and experimentation conducted by Kahneman and Tversky throughout the years is very extensive, and some of it is outside the scope of this book. There are, however, certain aspects of their research that are very relevant to financial behavior, and to the link between our decision-making process and our behavior. I would like to discuss some of these observations because they are very relevant in part two of this book when I outline the principles of the behavioralogy matrix.

System 1, the fast thinking mode, which stems from the instinctive and emotional functions of the brain, is responsible for making intuitive decisions very quickly and effortlessly. We share this thinking mode with our ancestors, as well as with many animals, because it alerts us to looming danger and promotes our most basic need—survival. For example, when the weather forecast warns of the approach of a big storm, we instinctively know to buy extra supplies such as food and water, and to make arrangements to protect ourselves and our property. Our instinctive decision to store food and water is no different from our ancestors' decision to hoard food and wood when they saw the first signs of bad weather. Of course our ancestors did not have the luxury of a weather forecast, but their senses were much sharper than ours, and they could detect looming storms by observing the elements and the behavior of animals.

Because System 1 is intuitive and does not require intellectual effort, we can conduct several such functions simultaneously. For example, we can decide to purchase an item marked down on sale vs. a similar item at a full retail price, and all this while we are thinking of how nice we look wearing this clothing item. These two tasks are effortless and easy to conduct. If the discounted price of the clothing item is $15, and the full retail price of the similar item is $50, it does not take much effort to figure out we are saving money buying the item on sale. Similarly, imagining yourself wearing this clothing item is effortless. In other words, our capacity to pay attention is sufficient to carry these two functions simultaneously.

On the other hand, System 2 requires mental effort and we can perform only one such complex task at a time because it requires our intellectual thinking. For example, try filling out your tax return and simultaneously figuring out the money you will save if you refinance your mortgage at 25 basis points lower than what you currently have. Clearly, you will have to perform each of these tasks separately because they require the use of the intellectual function of your brain that can focus its attention on one complex task at a time.

There is a clear division of labor between System 1 and System 2, which makes the interaction between the two systems very efficient and maximizes brain performance. System 1 is constantly on in full capacity while System 2 is on standby in case a complex thinking or calculation is needed. System 1 constantly feeds suggestive instincts, impulses and observations into System 2, which when needed, kicks into action to make an intellectual decision. We all experience this interaction in our daily lives. Take for example a visit to the grocery store where we observe the highly tempting candy bar at the checkout line. Our instinctive thought is how delicious the chocolate bar tastes and how good it will make us feel, but then, in most cases, our intellectual thinking reminds us that if we eat such candies, we might not fit into the new clothes we just purchased at a great discount. Such interaction between our instinctive and intellectual thinking is a common occurrence throughout our lives.

The division of labor between System 1 and System 2 of our brain functions is so evident in our day-to-day lives that each of us is practicing it, without always knowing we do. Here is an example from my own experience. As you can tell by now, I spend a substantial part of my time conducting research and analysis. When I am in my home office conducting financial analysis I feel that every once in a while that I need to get up and do something else; maybe listen to music, rearrange my desk or yes, even visit the refrigerator. Up until I started my research into behavioral economics and the theory of System 1 and System 2, I did not understand why I need to take such breaks from high-intensity thinking and do something that does not require deep analytical thinking. But now that I know, it all makes sense—our System 2 cannot keep going at high capacity for too long; it needs to cool down for a while before resuming activity.

Regardless of your occupation or profession, you probably do the same. Just think back to your activities that require high concentration and mental capacity—how long can you go before you feel the need to switch to a low-level mental capacity such as rearranging the items on your desk for the gazillionth time? Now you know it's not because you are lazy, unmotivated or a procrastinator, it's simply because this is how we are all built, which is one of the central ideas in this book—we behave the way we are built, not the other way around.

The main point of this discussion on System 1 and System 2 is that our two modes of thinking are tied to the makeup of our brain—System 1, fast and effortless thinking, originates in our instinctive or emotional functions of the brain; whereas System 2, the analytical and slower mode of thinking, originates in our intellectual function of the brain. The connection between our thinking mode and our brain function is evident in our financial behavior. In part two of this book, I will demonstrate how we default to System 1, our instinctive thinking mode, in times of economic uncertainty because the reptilian part of the brain was designed to make quick decisions to help us avoid immediate dangers. On the other hand, System 2, which is our analytical and slow thinking mode, is associated with our neocortex, allowing deeper analytical thinking during unthreatening economic times.

Hoarding Food and Wood

I named this chapter "human nature never changes" because after doing all the research for this book and conducting the analysis, I realized that our financial behavior today is no different than the behavior of our ancestors who faced uncertainty of survival, threatened by the elements and predatory animals. Since they did not have our understanding of the weather system and our ability to monitor storms, our ancestors lived in constant uncertainty about such natural phenomena, and their only defense was hoarding food for nutrition and wood to keep warm.

Our financial behavior today is no different than our ancestors' behavior—the only thing that changed over the years is the backdrop, from the scenic view of the elements to the panic view of Wall Street. Our biggest fear today and our main cause for uncertainty is the economy. Since we have an economic cycle of boom and bust every ten years on average, it turns out that every age group, from Gen Y to baby boomers, has experienced at least two recessions and recoveries in their lifetime. Thus every segment of the population has been exposed to the uncertainty of the economy.

Let's take a quick look at the economic cycles we went through just during the last 50 years to understand the impact such volatility has on people's financial anxiety. Clearly, not all economic cycles are alike. Some recessions are deeper and longer than others, and some recoveries are longer and slower than others. In reviewing the recessions we had in the last 50 years, I am going to use the official start and end dates of each recession, even though in actuality recessions start at least six months prior to the official declaration of the recession, and recoveries can take many years beyond the official end date.

We experienced a recession in the 1960s that lasted from April 1960 to February 1961. Not a very long recession and recovery was relatively fast. Then we had the recession at the end of the 1960s and the beginning of the1970s, which started in December of 1969 and ended in November 1970. Here, again, a relatively short recession and recovery was moderate. The 1970s had a second recession that started in November 1973 and ended in March 1975. This recession was relatively severe and recovery took a long time. As soon as the 1980s rolled around we had another recession, which started in January 1980 and lasted until November 1982; nearly two years. This recession was the most severe we had up until the Great Recession. The 1990s had a short and mild recession, which started in August 1990 and ended in March 1991, followed by another relatively mild recession that started in March 2001 and ended in November of the same year. And last but not least, the Great Recession, which officially started in December 2007 and officially ended in June 2008. By far, the Great Recession was the most severe since the Great Depression, and the slowest to recover—so far.

The main point I am trying to make here is that the economy, just like the elements, is cyclical; and because we don't always understand or predict economic cycles, it causes us anxiety. Since it is impossible to have absolute and complete control over a free market economy, the element of uncertainty will always be with us—there is no way around it. The only thing we can do to reduce the level of uncertainty and resulting anxiety is to learn how to measure consumer financial anxiety, which acts as a barometer for economic health. If we are successful in measuring and detecting shifts in consumer financial anxiety, we can take corrective action that could soften or shorten the severity and length of future economic cycles.

Chapter Two

Measuring Financial Anxiety

Financial anxiety is different from clinical anxiety, which is in the realm of psychiatry. In the context of behavioral economics, financial anxiety is a normal human reaction to varying economic conditions based on impulsive and cognitive functions of our brain. As we saw earlier in this book, our instinctive function of the brain, the one in charge of our survival, is the oldest function of our brain, and the most dominant when it comes to survival issues. Survival, of course, can mean actual physical survival, or in the context of this book, financial survival. In other words, when we feel or perceive any type of economic danger, we react as if there is a danger to our financial survival.

In order to understand the concept of financial anxiety, I would like to refer back to the root cause of financial anxiety, which is as old as mankind. Our ancestors, who lived in constant uncertainty about their next meal and their physical safety, reacted by hoarding food and wood to protect themselves from danger. Today's uncertainty is more financially oriented than physically, but the way we react to economic uncertainty activates the same instinct of hoarding in preparation for the worst. Hence, the link between financial anxiety and spending and savings that I will empirically demonstrate in this chapter.

The role of increased financial anxiety in the woes of the economy was cited by Yale economist Robert Shiller in an interview on September 2011 on "Wealthtrack" with reporter Consuelo Mack. According to Professor Shiller, a major reason for the sluggish economy and deteriorating housing market is a *social epidemic that feeds into our anxiety.*" He suggested that *"in the mind there is anxiety"* that holds people back from buying houses and increasing consumption. Moreover, Professor Shiller pointed to financial anxiety as a major factor in the stock market volatility, and he foresaw *"a substantial drop in stock prices. I am talking big, especially with the anxiety."*

It's very encouraging to see a top economist recognize the role that financial anxiety plays in the direction of the economy. The link between the level of financial anxiety and the economy is very strong and significant, and the more we recognize and utilize consumer financial anxiety in economic and financial models, the greater our ability to understand and project shifts in economic conditions.

Savings and Spending

Savings and spending are the two main pillars of the economy. Just their sheer size gives us an idea of the role they play in the economy. Currently, total government-insured deposits amount to about $12 trillion (yes, with a "T"). Of that, about $10.8 trillion is accumulated in bank deposits, insured by the FDIC (Federal Deposit Insurance Corporation), and about $1.2 trillion in credit union deposits, insured by the National Credit Union Administration, a U.S. government agency. Consumer spending, as we will soon see, is the engine of the economy, making up nearly 70% of Gross National Product, or GDP. A logical question would be: why are savings and spending so critical to the economy? The simple answer is that no free economy can exist without these two elements, and no healthy economy can be sustained without adequate levels of savings and spending. Let's look at the role and importance of savings and spending separately and then associate them together with financial anxiety.

When we think of savings, we have a mental picture of a child inserting coins into a piggy bank. That's a nice metaphor for savings, but the reality of savings is much greater in scope and importance. Savings is a key driver of the economy because it provides the capital needed for lending. Without lending, or credit, there can be hardly any business activity because it is nearly impossible for a new business to start generating operational profit from day one. Usually it takes a new business months (if they are lucky) or years to start generating operational profit to cover their expenses. Until such time, the business needs borrowed capital to operate. Another major use of consumer savings is for personal lending. Two of the main personal lending areas are mortgages and auto loans, which are the most common loans banks and credit unions provide.

I am purposely excluding equity capital from this scenario because even companies that were successful in obtaining equity capital needed some level of lending before they reached a level where they could show some ability to generate profit in the future. Thus, reaching a stage where a business can start raising equity capital either from private or public sources requires borrowing money from commercial banks, which is the source of capital in most cases.

Aside from the capital needed to finances businesses, there is the need for personal financing. Lending such as mortgages, car loans, personal loans and the like are mostly funded by commercial banks and credit unions. The capital for such loans, personal or business, comes from savings that are deposited in the bank or credit union. Without such savings, which are called deposits in the banking world, loans cannot be made. Moreover, since banks and credit unions are highly regulated, the amount they are allowed to lend depends on the level of deposits they have, which establishes their liquidity level.

The Federal Deposit Insurance Corporation (FDIC), which is a governmental agency, has very specific guidelines for the amount banks can lend, based on their liquidity level. The formula for determining the level of needed liquidity is a bit complex because it depends on the risk level of the loan portfolio of the bank, but for simplicity's sake let's say that banks can lend $100 for every $10 they have in deposits. Thus, if a bank wants to lend $200, they must have at least $20 in deposits. Moreover, a major part of these deposits must come from retail consumer deposits, not from other sources. These rules were established to ensure that a bank has enough capital to cover the risk level associated with the type of loans it makes.

You probably heard of the Basel I, in which central bankers from around the world, who formed the Committee on Banking Supervision (BCBS) in Basel, Switzerland, published a set of minimum capital requirements for banks. After the financial crisis that started in 2007, a more comprehensive set of guidelines, known as Basel II, has been established, requiring banks to increase their level of capital as a protection against a repeat of the last decade. As of the writing of this book, Basel III, which introduces new capital regulations, was just approved and is taking effect, requiring banks to increase the ratio of deposits to loans they extend to consumers.

Back to savings. Without the money that consumers deposit in the bank there will be no lending, which means that most people will not be able to buy homes, cars or any other major item, and businesses will not be able to start or expand. Clearly, an economy without savings is not going to survive. However, savings is a double-edge sword. It is good when people save because it provides a financial security in times of need, and liquidity for lending; yet too much of it is harmful to the economy because it prevents some money from circulating in and stimulating the economy.

Let's look more deeply at why too much savings are not good for the economy. Currently, at the time I am writing this book, the total amount of money consumers have in their bank and credit union accounts exceeds $12 trillion—about $10.8 trillion in banks, and about $1.2 trillion in credit union accounts. Do these figures look familiar? They should; because, as indicated above, consumer spending is at about $10.8 trillion, which means that as much money as all consumers in the US spend on consumption in one year is now sitting idle in bank accounts. And since money can't be in two places at a time, this means that every dollar sitting in bank accounts is one dollar less circulating and stimulating the economy.

Clearly, I do not advocate that people take all their money out of their savings accounts and spend it; but as we will see shortly, a certain amount of it, probably 20% or $2 trillion in the current scenario, was added to savings due to financial anxiety. These dollars might have been circulating in and stimulating the economy, had consumers' financial anxiety been lower. Just to put this in prospective, this amount is greater than the two stimulus programs the government and the Fed put in place in the form of Quantities Easing I & II.

I would like to clarify that "savings" in the context of this book refers to true savings in bank accounts and not what the government measures as "personal savings" in their various financial publications through the Bureau of Economic Analysis. The government's figure for personal savings is a deductive figure, which means that they arrive at the amount of personal savings by deducting spending and taxes from personal income. Clearly, that's not true savings because this method assumes that any amount left after spending and taxes is designated for savings, which is a subjective assumption. True savings measurement is the amount people actually deposit in their various bank accounts. Such measurement is objective and reliable because banks are required to report the exact amount of consumers' deposits to the FDIC. Thus, when referring to savings in this book, I am referring to the actual official figure for total money deposited in insured bank and credit union deposit accounts.

Now let's look at the other driver of the economy: consumer spending, or as officially called in governmental reports, Personal Consumption Expenditures. Consumer spending is the sum total of money consumers spend on goods and services during a one-year period. The reason consumer spending is so critical to the US economy is that it makes up about 70% of the Gross Domestic Product (GDP). The remaining 30% is made up of government spending —about 20%—and investments—about 10%.

This fact alone is enough to demonstrate the importance of consumer spending to the overall economy. The way consumers feel about the economy, which is their level of financial anxiety, can make or break the economy. When consumers feel confident about their current economic standing and the prospect for future economic improvement, they tend to spend more, which stimulates the economy by increasing demand for goods and services, which in return, creates jobs in order to satisfy the demand. On the other hand, when the level of consumer financial anxiety grows due to diminishing buying power, rising unemployment and uncertainty about their future finances, consumers tend to halt spending, which reduces demand for goods and services, resulting in layoffs due to declining demand.

It's obvious why savings and spending are the two pillars of the economy. Current savings, at about $12 trillion, and spending, currently about $11.4 trillion, are substantial relative to GDP. Moreover, the fact that the current level of savings, at about $12 trillion, is greater than our annual consumption amount of $11.4 trillion is an indication of some uncertainty and therefore anxiety over the economy. These two figures alone should place the Money Anxiety Index at the top of the list of economic indicators for economists and analysts because, as we will see shortly, the level of consumer financial anxiety is strongly associated with the level of consumer savings and spending.

Money Anxiety Index

Financial anxiety is one of those elusive variables that statisticians call latent variables because they cannot be directly observed or measured. So how do we measure something we can't observe? Fortunately, the science of statistics has provided a solution to this challenge. Since financial anxiety can't be directly observed, we can observe it indirectly by measuring its impact on other variables—in our case savings and spending. For those of you who are statistically inclined, the statistical model used to measure financial anxiety as a latent variable is Structural Equation Modeling (SEM).

When I started exploring the notion that financial anxiety plays a major role in consumer financial behavior, back in the early 2000s, I did not realize how complex and lengthy this process was going to be. It's relatively easy to measure relations between variables we can measure and observe, such as unemployment and inflation, but how do we measure a state of mind? Fairly early in the process, I ruled out the use of consumer surveys because I discovered that what people say they do and what they actually do can be two different things. I will elaborate on this phenomenon and provide evidence of the gap between what consumers say in response to questionnaires and what they actually do with their money in the next chapter. For now, I want to explain why I chose the path of discovery rather than settling for the status quo of asking consumers how they feel about the economy.

Since I could not find any previous work in this area, I started by designing the model, which basically establishes consumer savings and spending as the two dependent variables (in Structural Equation Modeling you can have more than one dependent variable), every major economic indicator as the independent variable, and of course, consumer financial anxiety as an intervening variable. Since there are a few dozen major economic indicators, such as inflation, unemployment, personal consumption and the like, I had my work cut out for me in going through an exhaustive trial and error process. The basic principle in this process is to find the combination of major economic indicators that impact consumer savings and spending through the intervention of financial anxiety, and all while producing the required measurement of fit for the model. Since the scope of this book is not statistical modeling, suffice to say that the Money Anxiety Index satisfies all the measurement of fit for the Structural Equation Modeling. In other words, it works.

Another major consideration in the development of the Money Anxiety Index was the use of the largest data set I could find in order to eliminate the possibility of sample error. So I used the largest data set available from various governmental sources starting in January of 1959—over 50 years of economic data. This large data set allowed me to clearly see how consumer financial anxiety fluctuated through seven different economic cycles of recessions and recovery. Moreover, the use of such large data set allowed me to observe variations in the levels of consumer financial anxiety among the various recessions, and to establish the highest and lowest points of consumer financial anxiety over the past 50 years. In a nutshell, the Money Anxiety Index spans from January 1959 to date, and it fluctuated from a high of 135.3 during the recession of the early 1980s to a low of 38.7 in the mid-1960s. The 50-year average is 70.7, and July 1980 is the index's baseline of 100.

Just about the time the Great Recession began (officially December of 2007), I started observing how the amounts of money people save and spend were reversing course compared to other periods in which the economy was doing well, and the level of consumer financial anxiety was relatively low. This observation made sense because it matched normal human behavior, which in this case means that in times of economic uncertainty, i.e. lack of job security, upside-down mortgages, and volatile stock market, the survival instinct kicks in and we react by reducing spending and putting the money in the bank, where it is safe because it is federally insured.

In order to demonstrate the contrast between consumer financial behaviors during times of low financial anxiety compared to times of high financial anxiety, I analyzed two five-year periods. I am presenting the variance in percentage because it is simpler to see the contrast, and also because when using percentage, the impact of other variables, such as growth in population, inflation and others is neutralized. Thus, the relative increase or decrease in the variables is a true representation of the actual change.

Percentage change in money anxiety, spending and savings

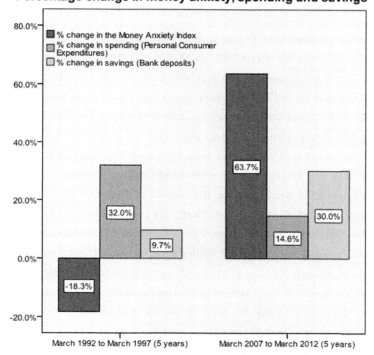

Source: BEA, FDIC and moneyanxiety.com

The first time period is from March 1992 to March 1997, when the Money Anxiety Index was relatively low. During this five-year period, the Money Anxiety Index decreased by 18.3%, which means that the level of financial anxiety decreased, and people were feeling more financially secure. During the same time period, the amount of consumers' spending, also known as Consumer Expenditure (or PCE), increased by 32.0%.

One does not have to be an economist to figure out that during times of low financial anxiety, consumers tend to spend more because they have greater confidence about the future, i.e. that tomorrow they will still have their jobs and be able to pay for the purchases they made today or yesterday. When it comes to savings, consumers still put money aside in their bank accounts, an increase of 9.7% during the five-year period, which is less than one-third of the amount they saved during high-financial anxiety periods.

Now let's compare that to consumer financial behavior during the five-year period from March of 2007 to March of 2012. This time period covers the Great Recession, which was officially declared on December 2007, and officially ended in June 2009, as well as the years following the official end of the Great Recession, the so-called "recovery" period.

During this five-year period, consumer financial anxiety increased by 63.7%, which means that consumers were very worried about their financial future (and still are at the time of writing this book). Again, no economic background is needed to see the impact of high-financial anxiety on spending, which declined by more than half compared to the five-year period of low financial anxiety—from 32.0% down to 14.6%. Clearly, consumers were holding back on some spending as a natural and instinctive reaction to uncertainty. On the other hand, consumers piled up money in savings, which again is a natural and instinctive reaction to economic uncertainty. Savings in bank accounts grow more than three times the rate as in times of low financial anxiety—from 9.7% to 30.0%.

Keep in mind that the motivation for increasing savings was not the desire to gain interest on this money, but rather the safety and security of the Federal Deposit Insurance Corporation (FDIC). We know that getting high yield on these deposits was not the motivation because according to the FDIC, the average interest rate on all bank deposit at the time of writing is less than one half of one percent. Nearly enough to buy a cup of coffee a year on a $1,000 deposit (Grande Cappuccino, which is about $5, and yes, with tip you are actually losing money on your deposit).

Ironically, just as I was writing this section of the book, the U.S. Census Bureau released the advance estimates of U.S. retail and food services sales for March 2013, showing a decrease of 0.4 percent from February of this year. This came as a surprise to many people because the feeling was that the economy is improving somewhat due to lower unemployment rate, which decreased to 7.6 in March of 2013. As you will see later on in the book, the decline in retail sales is not a coincidence—it is precisely the result of high level of consumer financial anxiety. In the second part of this book, I demonstrate empirically the link between the two.

What About Investing?

Often I am asked "can the Money Anxiety Index predict the stock market?" The simple answer is yes and no. Here is what I mean. The money Anxiety Index is a monthly index, and therefore it can't be associated with daily fluctuations in the stock market. However, the Money Anxiety Index is capable of detecting macro trends in consumer financial anxiety, which is useful in making longer term strategic investment decisions rather than daily tactical decisions to buy or sell individual stocks.

Here is a case in point. The Money Anxiety Index warned of irrational confidence in its August analysis right after a stock market rally based on the increase in reported consumer confidence. The stock market rally pushed the DJIA over the 13,000 mark for the first time since the recession started in late 2007, and it reached its highest, at that time, post-recession level of 13,596 on September 20, 2012. At that time, the Money Anxiety Index pointed to an increasing level of financial anxiety and lo and behold, the DJIA started its decline of 1,008 points when it closed at 12,588 on Friday, the 16th of November 2012.

The August 2012 analysis by the Money Anxiety Index indicated that underneath the improving job figures and the reported increase in consumer confidence there was a growing financial nervousness and anxiety among consumers. The Money Anxiety Index noted that the Dow Jones Industrial Average was due for a correction once economic reality sank in, which occurred in mid-September when the DJIA started its decline of 7.4 percent up until Friday November 16, 2012. Here is what Jeff Cox, senior writer for CNBC.com wrote about my analysis on Monday August 6, 2012:

Money Anxiety Index:
Stock Market Rally 'Totally Irrational'

The stock market rally worth about 300 points on the Dow over the past three sessions is "totally irrational," according to the curator of the Money Market Index economic barometer.

In particular, investor enthusiasm over Friday's monthly jobs report from the government is misplaced because a large portion of the 163,000 new non-farm jobs reported are temporary and likely to vanish soon, says Dan Geller, chief research officer of the index.

"The rally on Friday after the release of the employment figures and the consumer confidence index really has no economic merit," Geller says. "It's totally irrational."

When formulating the Money Market Index, Geller looks to more lasting attributes.

Specifically, he places a large weight on Personal Consumer Expenditures, which have been flat for two months. Another measure in the index, gross domestic product, registered an anemic 1.5 percent growth in the second quarter.

The index also factors in spending and saving numbers. Recent government data showed spending is flat while saving appears to be increasing.

The index is registering a 2012 high of 92.0 that, while lower than the same period last year, is indicative of worsening conditions.

Bottom line: the Money Anxiety Index is a highly predictable barometer of the level of consumer financial anxiety and can point to trends in consumer financial behavior ahead of conventional consumer confidence indices because it measures actual behavior rather than the stated opinions of consumers. In the next chapter on the "confidence gap" between what consumers say and what they actually do, I will demonstrate how the Money Anxiety Index predicted the Great Recession and the market crash a few months prior to any such indication by conventional consumer confidence indices.

Chapter Three

Are we doing what we are saying?

Consumer Confidence Indices

Incorporating consumer confidence data in economic and financial projections is a common practice among analysts and economists. But what does it really tell us when consumer confidence shows an increase or a decrease? Not much. In reality, consumer confidence is not a measurement of what consumers actually do; rather it is what they say about the economy that gets recorded and reported. Therefore, it is important that we distinguish between two types of data: "hard" and "soft". Hard data is based on actual observations of specific occurrences such as consumers' level of savings and spending. The data is objective because only actual observations that occurred in reality are included. Soft data, on the other hand, is based on what consumers say in response to questionnaires, such as a consumer confidence survey. In this case, the respondent reports what he or she thinks about the economy, which is completely subjective because it is an opinion and not on observed action.

There are various entities that collect and publish consumer confidence data on a monthly basis, which I will briefly cover in this section. The main point to keep in mind is that all of them, without exception, are based on responses from consumers—meaning that they are subjective in nature and should be regarded as such. I will demonstrate how subjective data on consumer confidence is not always reflective of the actual economic reality, and how an objective measurement, such as the Money Anxiety Index, is capable of detecting changes in the economy because it is based on what consumers actually do, not what they say they do.

The two most widely followed indices of consumer confidence are the Conference Board's Consumer Confidence Index and the Thomson Reuters/University of Michigan Index of Consumer Sentiment, which was previously called the University of Michigan's Consumer Sentiment Index, or in short, UMCSENT. These two indices are regularly cited in financial publications and broadcasts. The Conference Board publishes its monthly Consumer Confidence Index in the last week of each calendar month, whereas the Thomson Reuters/University of Michigan Index of Consumer Sentiment is published twice a month—preliminary results in mid-month, and final results at month end.

The Conference Board Consumer Confidence Index

The Conference Board measurement of consumer confidence is based on a survey of 5,000 households, of which about 3,000 or so typically respond on a monthly basis. The index started in 1967, and has been updated monthly ever since. The year 1985 was established as the baseline for the index at 100 points because it represented neither a peak nor a trough in confidence. The Conference Board uses the Nielsen Company as the survey provider. Nielsen uses a mail survey specifically designed for the Consumer Confidence Survey. The index is calculated each month based on questions regarding the five following areas:

1. Respondents' appraisal of current business conditions
2. Respondents' expectations regarding business conditions six months hence
3. Respondents' appraisal of the current employment conditions
4. Respondents' expectations regarding employment conditions six months hence

5. Respondents' expectations regarding their total family income six months hence

Each of the five questions has three response options: positive, negative and neutral. The positive responses are divided by the sum of the positive and negative responses to form a proportion, which is then compared to the average proportions from the base year of 1985 to create an index value. The answers to all five questions form the basis for the Consumer Confidence Index, which means that expectations have a 60 percent weight in the headline measure, while assessment of the present situation comprises a 40 percent share. The answers to questions 1 and 3 make up the Present Situation Index, while questions 2, 4 and 5 are used for the Expectations Index.

Since the Consumer Confidence Index started in 1967, it has recorded an average of about 94 (as of the writing of this book). Its highest point of 144.7 was recorded in January 2000 and its lowest point at 25.3 during the recession of 2009.

Thomson Reuters/University of Michigan Index of Consumer Sentiment

Another frequently cited consumer confidence index is the Thomson Reuters/University of Michigan Index of Consumer Sentiment (ICS). This index is published jointly by Michigan University and Thomson Reuters. The sample used in this index is only 500 households surveyed by phone, which is much smaller than the Conference Board's 5,000 household sample size. The telephone survey asks a number of questions, of which the following five are used to calculate the Consumer Sentiment Index:

1. We are interested in how people are getting along financially these days. Would you say that you (and your family living there) are better off or worse off financially than you were a year ago?

2. Now looking ahead--do you think that a year from now you (and your family living there) will be better off financially, or worse off, or just about the same as now?

3. Now turning to business conditions in the country as a whole--do you think that during the next twelve months we'll have good times financially, or bad times, or what?

4. Looking ahead, which would you say is more likely--that in the country as a whole we'll have continuous good times during the next five years or so, or that we will have periods of widespread unemployment or depression, or what?

5. About the big things people buy for their homes--such as furniture, a refrigerator, stove, television, and things like that. Generally speaking, do you think now is a good or bad time for people to buy major household items?

The Index of Consumer Sentiment is part of the Survey of Consumers, which is a rotating panel survey based on a nationally representative sample that gives each household in the contiguous states an equal chance of being included. According to the University of Michigan, the minimum monthly change required for significance at the 95 percent level in the Sentiment Index is 4.8 points; for Current and Expectations Index the minimum is 6.0 points.

Subjective vs. Objective Confidence

This principle of subjective vs. objective confidence, or soft vs. hard data as we discussed earlier, is very straightforward, yet many economists and analysts ignore this distinction when it comes to economic analysis and forecasting. By now we understand that there are times when there is a difference between what people say and what they actually do financially, and in other aspects of life as well. The following case in point illustrates the difference between what consumers say and what they actually do in financial matters. I am going to use an example from the last recession because this event is still fresh in our minds, and we can all relate to it.

As we discussed in earlier chapters, when people are financially anxious, they are much more likely to cut back on discretional spending; and vice versa: when people feel financially confident, they are much more likely to increase spending. On that basis, the only way we can have an increase in consumer confidence and a decrease in consumer spending at the same time is if there is a discrepancy between what consumers say and what they actually do. This means that consumers say they are confident about the economy, but in reality they are reducing their spending due to financial anxiety caused by the economic uncertainty. Remember that confidence and high financial anxiety are opposite ends of the economic spectrum, and they can't occur simultaneously.

Also, keep in mind that the Money Anxiety Index behaves inversely to other consumer confidence indices. In other words, a higher number on the consumer confidence indices denotes a higher confidence level, whereas a higher number on the Money Anxiety Index denotes higher financial anxiety. Therefore, when comparing these two types of indices, higher confidence is the equivalent of lower anxiety level and vice versa.

A notable discrepancy between what consumers reported to the Thomson Reuters/University of Michigan Index of Consumer Sentiment and what they actually did financially occurred between October 2006 and January of 2007—the time period leading to the Great Recession. In the four months between October 2006 and January 2007, the Thomson Reuters/University of Michigan Index of Consumer Sentiment reported an increase in consumer confidence from 93.6 to 96.9—an increase of 3.3 index points, indicating a significant increase in consumer confidence.

However, during the same time period, the U.S. Department of Commerce, Bureau of Economic Analysis, reported that the monthly growth in real personal consumption expenditure (fancy term for consumer spending) decreased from 0.5% in October of 2006 to 0.1% in January of 2007. This basically means that consumers started slowing down on spending during the same time period when consumers reported a higher confidence level to the Thomson Reuters/University of Michigan Index of Consumer Sentiment. Clearly, there is a disconnect between these two incidents because highly confident consumers don't just reduce spending so drastically. By the way, a month later in February of 2007, the percentage change was zero, i.e. growth in spending came to a halt.

Now let's take a look at the Money Anxiety Index over the same time period. Between October 2006 and January 2007, the Money Anxiety Index started showing signs of an increasing level of financial anxiety from 52.5 to 56.5—an increase of 4 index points, which is a substantial rise in financial anxiety over such a short time period. This trend corresponds with and supports the slowdown in consumer spending reported by the U.S. Department of commerce. Moreover, it shows that consumers started getting anxious about the economy, and *de facto* reduced their spending, a few months before they said so to pollsters of the Thomson Reuters/University of Michigan Index of Consumer Sentiment.

The two charts below clearly demonstrate the gap between what consumers say and what they actually do with their finances. In the top chart, you can see how the Thomson Reuters/University of Michigan Index of Consumer Sentiment is reporting an increase in consumer confidence all the way to the turning point in January of 2007, and only then starting to report a decrease in consumer confidence all the way to the official start of the Great Recession in December of 2007. Again, it is important to note that the Thomson Reuters/University of Michigan Index of Consumer Sentiment reports responses from consumers. Thus their report accurately reflected what consumers indicated in the questionnaire, but it clearly did not reflect the actual behavior of consumers, who were decreasing spending due to a higher level of financial anxiety about the economy.

The bottom chart reflects the Money Anxiety Index during the same time period. You can clearly see how the turning point in the level of consumer financial anxiety occurred in October of 2006—three months earlier than the turning point in the Thomson Reuters/University of Michigan Index of Consumer Sentiment. The increase in the Money

Anxiety Index starting in October of 2006 is consistent with the reports of the U.S. Department of Commerce, which indicated a decrease in the growth of retail sales from 0.5% in October of 2006 to 0.1% in January of 2007. In short, consumers' level of financial anxiety started rising in October of 2006, when they reduced their spending due to uncertainty about the state of the economy.

Thomson Reuters/University of Michigan Index of Consumer Sentiment

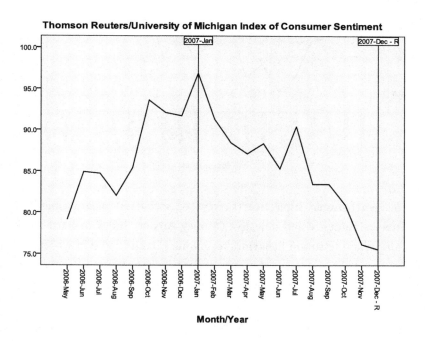

31

Money Anxiety Index

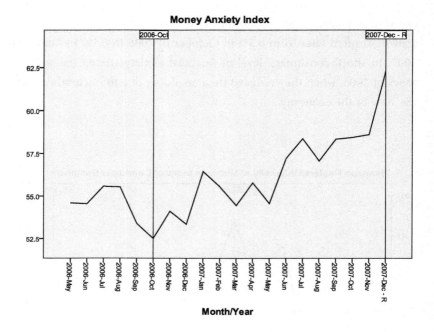

Month/Year

The gap between subjective (surveys or soft data) measurement of consumer confidence and objective (Money Anxiety Index or hard data) is an important lesson in behavioral economics. It showed that what people say about the economy, through surveys, is not always what they do with their finances in response to changing economic conditions. In this particular case, consumers reported higher confidence level, in response to questions in the Survey, than they actually felt. We can see that consumers started lowering their spending and increasing their savings level before they reported a lower confidence level to the Thomson Reuters/University of Michigan Index of Consumer Sentiment.

The observation of the confidence gap demonstrates that the economy is more fragile than we think because consumers start reacting to changes in economic conditions sooner than they tell us through surveys. Thus, in response to an increasing level of financial anxiety, consumers start slowing down their spending and increasing their savings, both of which put the brakes on the economy. In the following chapters, I will discuss what happens when consumers react to increasing financial anxiety by reducing consumption and increasing savings.

The Consumer Confidence Paradox

When it comes to survey-based consumer confidence reports, it looks as if you can be both—confident and not confident at the same time in the same place. At least that is how it appears in the January 2012 consumer confidence results by the two major consumer confidence indices—the Conference Board and the Thomson Reuters/University of Michigan Index of Consumer Sentiment.

The January 2012 Consumer Sentiment index, produced by Thompson Reuters/University of Michigan, reported an increase of 5.1 points from December 2011, whereas the Consumer Confidence Index, produced by the Conference Board, reported a decline of 3.7 points for the same month. Clearly, consumers' confidence in the economy cannot be increasing and decreasing at the same time in the same economy, which points to a deficiency in the concept of subjective surveys.

The conflicting results in the January 2012 indices between the Thomson Reuters/University of Michigan Index of Consumer Sentiment and The Conference Board Consumer Confidence Index are rooted in their reliance on what consumers are saying rather than on what consumers are doing, such as spending and savings levels. Such discrepancy occurs because people do not always say what they do, nor do they always do what they say. Hence, consumer confidence indices relaying on consumer responses are subjective, and are not as reliable as the Money Anxiety Index, which is completely objective because it is based only on real economic indicators.

The methodology both consumer confidence incises use is fairly similar with a few exceptions. Both surveys include five core questions regarding current and future economic conditions, and both use a relative weight to each of the questions. The main differences between the two surveys is that the Conference Board uses a mail survey to about 5,000

33

households (although only about 3,000 respond), whereas the Thompson Reuters/University of Michigan survey is done by phone to about 500 households.

The main takeaway here is that despite empirical evidence about the confidence gap between what consumers say and what they actually do, many economists and analysts are still using such subjective indices as a predictor of economic activities. One of the objectives of this book is to increase awareness of the confidence gap, and to encourage the use of objective measurement of consumer confidence such as the Money Anxiety Index, based on hard economic data, to gauge how consumers feel about the economy.

Economic Chicken and Egg

I thought a lot about the chicken and the egg dilemma as it pertains to consumer financial behavior and the economy. Just like the classic chicken and the egg dilemma, the question is—what came first, the chicken or the egg? Or—what comes first, consumer financial behavior or economic conditions? We know from previous chapters of this book and from our own personal experience that consumer financial behavior is closely linked to economic conditions. Each of us, assuming that we are over the age of ten, has experienced at least one cycle of economic growth and economic recession. This experience has impacted our financial behavior regardless of our financial status because economic booms and busts impact everyone to some degree.

Back to the question of what comes first, or which of the two is the cause and which one is the effect. If we say that consumer financial behavior comes first and therefore is the cause of economic conditions, then the next question is—what causes consumer financial behavior to change in the first place? If the answer is economic conditions come first and they are the cause of changes in consumer financial behavior, the next question is—what caused economic conditions to change? You see the dilemma?

After much deliberation and thought about the question of which came first, I reached the conclusion that the answer lies elsewhere—in physics. We are all familiar with the big bang theory. By now it is more than a theory because there is ample scientific evidence to support the notion that about 4.5 billion years ago there was a great release of energy that created all there is today. Let's assume for a minute that prior to the big bang there was nothing—pure nothingness—and therefore, nothing else could be claimed to be the cause of the big bang. Once the big bang occurred, it started a chain of reaction that led us to where we are today.

Now let's apply the same model to the interaction between consumer financial behavior and economic conditions. Let's assume that an independent event that is neither consumer behavior nor economic conditions occurs, and it triggers consumers to change their financial behavior, thus impacting economic conditions. If that is the case, what is this independent event that is causing the change in consumer financial behavior? One possibility is rumors. Rumors have a tendency to spread very fast, especially today in the age of instant and vast interactivity through social media and the Internet. When a rumor is believed by enough people, it can transform itself into reality purely by critical mass.

Once an independent event such as a rumor occurs, consumers start to change their financial behavior to prepare for whatever financial challenges they anticipate as a result of the rumor. For example, we all know that to some degree companies outsource some part of their operations. But if a rumor circulates about large number of companies planning on outsourcing most of their operations overseas in the next 12 months, and enough people believe it, we are very likely to see a consumer financial reaction to this rumor, and anticipation of higher unemployment. You will see later on in this book how a major part of consumer financial anxiety is caused by anticipation of economic conditions, not necessarily by current economic conditions. This means that even though currently there is no increase in the unemployment rate, the anticipation of an increase in the unemployment rate is enough to cause consumers to spend less and save more in preparation for a possible loss of job.

A classic example of how rumors can trigger a chain reaction that activates consumer financial anxiety, which in turn impacts the economy, occurred on April 23, 2013, when computer hackers hacked into the Twitter account of Associated Press and tweeted a bogus message. Here is the report from NBC News: *"Following a hack attack, the Associated Press' verified Twitter account posted 'an erroneous tweet' claiming that two explosions occurred in the White House and that President Barack Obama is injured. Moments later, the @AP Twitter account—with nearly 2 million followers—was suspended. Immediately following the false tweet, the Dow Industrial Average lost about 140 points. These losses were immediately recovered."*

As you can see, consumers reacted right away to rumors of danger and sold stock in anticipation of an economic slowdown or bust. Since this rumor was dispelled right away, the financial damage was minimal. However, had this incident taken longer to correct, consumers' reaction could have had severe consequences on the stock market and possibly impacted bank savings and consumer spending as well.

Part Two

Behavioralogy – The Science of Financial Behavior

Mattress Money	Durable Diet
Power Play	Tiny Treats
Rate Race	Castle Craze

Behavioralogy is the DNA of consumer financial behavior.

Chapter Four

Consumer Segmentation and Orientation

The practice of identifying consumers' unique attributes and segmenting them into groups is not new. Basic demographic segmentation has been around for decades. In the early 1990s, a new type of segmentation was introduced—typology or psychographics, which segmented people by their type, such as achievers, followers and the like. Psychographic segmentation added another dimension to our understanding of consumer behavior and our attempt to better understand and anticipate how people are likely to act based on known associations between attributes and behavior. However, even the addition of psychographic attributes to demographic segmentation did not address the main deficiency of such segmentation models—lack of behavioral orientation, which is independent of consumer demographic or psychographic classification.

Demographics and Psychographics

Demographic segmentation is a method used to segment people according to their income, age, gender, education and the like, and psychographic segmentation segments people by their type, such as achievers, survivors etc. These two segmentation methods define people in accordance to static attributes. For example, if a study shows that males are more likely to buy goods in bulk quantities than females, we have associated economic activities with each of the two gender segments—male and female. However, in Behavioralogy the behavior of each of these gender segments can vary based on changing economic conditions, which is why I use the term orientation rather than segmentation. Orientation, unlike segmentation, is a relative term, which is used in psychology to describe the ability to locate oneself in one's changing environment as it relates to places, situations or people. Therefore, Behavioralogy is an orientation because its measurement is fluid and fluctuates relative to changes in economic conditions.

Behavioralogy considers consumers as a homogeneous group—with no pre-defined demographic or psychographic segments—which modifies its financial behavior based on varying economic conditions. It does not matter what level of education consumers have or their age; these consumers will most likely behave in the same financial pattern when exposed to similar economic conditions. It's the consumers' orientation that changes with economic conditions, not the consumers themselves. Granted, there are variations in the degree of financial behavior among consumers based on economic means and financial ability, but the financial behavior in and of itself, as we will see soon, is identical regardless of demographic or psychographic affiliation.

Let's assume, for example, that a company is in the process of layoffs, and the current unemployment rate is very high. Would the financial behavior of employees with varying degrees of income, age or education differ as far as reduction in normal spending and/or increase in savings? The answer is no. It is very likely that most people facing such financial circumstances will behave in the same way—they will reduce spending and increase savings. Why? Because these two actions come from the same part of the brain, which we all have—the instinctive brain that controls our desire for survival.

We are creatures of habit. We do things because we have always done them in a certain way, and because we are programmed to react to situations in a particular manner. The same goes for the way we like to view the world and the people in it—we like to compartmentalize everything into defined groups so that we can understand and explain occurrences by association. A classic example of our need for compartmentalization is demographic segmentation, probably one of the oldest and most commonly used segmentation methods in use. We divide people into groups based on their income, age and gender so that we can target specific groups for business or social reasons. Demographic segmentation is a very useful tool because it allows us to narrow down the audience for our product, service or message. If we know that only a certain age group is likely to buy our product or service, then targeting the message to this group is the most effective way to get our message across to the right audience either for commercial or social reasons.

Demographic segmentation also helps us associate segments with activities. For example, if we know that people in the age range of 18 to 35 are the most likely to buy the latest electronic gadget, then we can associate this age group with the tendency to be more adventurous in trying new inventions. The same applies to income range, education level and gender. Some demographic associations are simpler than others. For example, it does not take much to figure out that females are the most likely group to buy cosmetic products, and that male consumers are the most likely to buy power tools. Yes, there are exceptions to both examples; but in any type of segmentation, the idea is to deal with the rule rather than the exception.

In reality, demographic segmentation tells us just half the story. It tells us what group consumers belong to based on their age, income, education or gender, but not necessarily who they are. For example, is it possible that some baby boomers will buy the same products as Gen Y, or that their spending level will be identical despite the age difference? Or that people of varying education level will buy the same financial product? Yes, absolutely. This phenomenon of cross-segment behavior created the need for a supplemental segmentation methodology called psychographic or typology.

Typology was introduced in the early 1980s, initially by Stanford Research Institution (SRI), later called Strategic Business Insights SBI), when they presented VALS—Value and Life Style segmentation. The concept behind the typology segmentation is that people have varying values and lifestyle traits regardless of basic demographic segmentation criteria. In other words, people can share the same values even if they don't share the same educational level, income or age group. The VALS segmentation is based on a database consisting of consumers' responses to an online survey. The survey contains 41 questions, some of which are objective, such as age, gender and educational level; but most of which are subjective questions in the form of a statement and a four-scale response from "mostly disagree" to "mostly agree" such as "I would rather make something than buy it." Just as a side note, a four-point response scale is not ideal because it does not provide respondents with a "neutral" option, when they don't feel strongly about agreeing or disagreeing with the provided statement. A five-point response scale is more accommodating to subjective questions.

According to Strategic Business Insights, "VALS™ segments U.S. adults into eight distinct types—or mindsets—using a specific set of psychological traits and key demographics that drive consumer behavior." These eight types are: Innovators, Thinkers, Believers, Achievers, Strivers, Experiencers, Makers and Survivors. For each of the eight types, Strategic Business Insights provides a description of the main values and lifestyle shared by people in the group. For example, Strategic Business Insights describes Survivors' behavior as: "Survivors are cautious consumers. They represent a very modest market for most products and services. They are loyal to favorite brands, especially if they can purchase them at a discount."

So the question is: how do psychographic researchers know that Survivors are loyal to a brand? The answer is because that's what Strategic Business Insights deducted from the responses people provided in their survey posted online. Here again, as in the case of the consumer confidence surveys we discussed earlier, we are faced with the same critical question: how do we know that the responses consumers provided in the survey match their actual behavior? Here, too, we encounter the same situation we uncovered with the consumer confidence indices—a potential discrepancy between what people say they do, and what they do in actuality.

There are only three ways to associate people with behavior. The first is an actual observation of the behavior, which provides the most reliable link between people and behavior. However, it is also the most difficult and complex method to conduct. For example, actually observing consumers making deposits into their money market bank accounts during decreasing levels of interest rates could provide a strong and reliable indication that the particular group of consumers is not sensitive to lower interest rates and is likely to keep on depositing funds into their bank accounts regardless of the interest rate that the bank is paying them.

The second type of associating people with behavior is by analyzing overall results. In this method of data collection, we associate overall behavior with economic variables. For example, if interest rates on car loans decline, and we observe an increase in car loan activity and in car purchase, then we can conclude that car purchasers are sensitive to interest rates on car loans, and that demand for cars will increase when interest rates on car loans decrease. This method of association is optimal because, although it does not provide actual observation of the behavior, it does provide reliable and empirical data that is objective rather than subjective.

The third and least credible association of consumers and behavior is the survey method, which is the most commonly used method in social science because it is the most cost effective, and because the survey questions can be designed specifically for the research questions. However, the survey methodology has some major deficiencies because, as we discussed earlier, it provides subjective data that is based on responses from consumers, and thus reflects what consumers reported as doing rather than objective observation of their actual behavior.

Behavioralogy—Behavioral Orientation

In the context of financial behavior, behavioral orientation means that consumers modify, or more precisely orient, their behavior relative to the economic conditions they are anticipating or currently facing. Such a change in behavioral orientation is done despite their attributes, which is the key difference between demographic or psychographic segmentation and behavioral orientation. Both demographic and psychographic segmentation operate under the premise that the behavior of each of the groups is static, and that each of the segments behaves as a cohort in a cohesive manner regardless of any changes in economic conditions.

Understanding consumer financial behavior is essential to any business regardless of the product or service they provide. The reason behavioral knowledge and insight is so important in business and finance is that it allows executives to anticipate the behavior of their consumers during varying economic times, in order to ensure that the types of products and services the company provides are likely to be desirable and attractive to consumers under the prevailing economic conditions. Let's look at a classic case of consumer behavior with a specific case of behavioral orientation.

During recessionary times, there is a drastic reduction in the sale of new automobiles. A quick glance at the "before and after" the Great Recession of 2007 to 2009 shows a dramatic decrease in the level of new car sales—a behavior that is consistent with recessionary times, and which I call prolonging. This behavior consists of prolonging or stretching the use of already existing products in use in order not to spend additional money during times of economic uncertainty. We can clearly see from the retail trade figures published by the U.S. Department of Commerce how this behavioral orientation impacted new car sales during the Great Recession. Automobile sales peaked in September 2007 at $72 billion, which was just a few months before the official declaration of the last recession in December of 2007. Since then, car sales decreased to a low of $47 billion in March 2009, which was at the tail end of the Great Recession. This reduction of 35 percent in car sales was not because people needed fewer cars, but rather because people postponed buying new cars until they felt the economy was improving, and basically kept on using their existing vehicles for a longer period than they would normally do during better economic times. As soon as the Great Recession officially ended in June of 2009 and the economy was slowly moving towards a recovery period car sales steadily increased, to a level of $71 billion as of December of 2012.

Fluctuation in economic conditions is an integral part of every economy, and if we know what to expect from customers' behavior during different stages of an economic cycle, we can plan to meet their needs during these specific times. Such preparation and foresight is instrumental to the long-term survival of any business. If a business is caught unprepared during a significant change in the financial behavior—or Behavioralogy—of its customers, these businesses are likely to incur severe financial loss and a decline in their customer base.

I will discuss in detail the application of Behavioralogy in the next few chapters of this book, but for now let's refer back to the example of the drastic decline in new car sales during recessionary times. Now that we know consumers are likely to prolong the use of their existing vehicles during recessionary economic times, how can manufacturers and dealers prepare for such circumstances, and how should they handle such changes in consumer financial behavior? For one thing, car manufacturers should plan on reducing production and inventories at the first signs of high financial anxiety, and focus on the production of more economic and highly reliable cars. When consumers are in the prolonging stage, they are looking for products that are less expensive and will last them a long time. At the same time, car dealers should ride out the prolonging stage by increasing incentives and promotion on servicing existing vehicles—a message that resonates well with consumers in search of ways to avoid spending money on a new car by prolonging the use of their existing one.

DAN GELLER, PH.D.

Economic "Seasons"

Much like the climate system in most of the world, a free-market economy has four seasons. We are all familiar with the two main seasons—economic growth and economic decline, which come and go every decade or so. In addition to these two main seasons, there are the two transitional seasons—which, like spring and fall, lead to the main season. Thus, before any period of economic growth there is a period of transition from the previous recession, and conversely before any period of economic decline there is a transitional period of economic slowdown.

If we look at the last decade, we can clearly see the four economic seasons in play, based on the level of consumers' financial anxiety. We started the year 2000 with a relatively strong economy. The unemployment rate was 4.0 percent and the level of financial anxiety was relatively low at 57.0. By August of 2000, we started the transitional period to the recession of 2001. Consumers' financial anxiety started to climb up, as did unemployment. By the time the official recession was declared in March of 2001, the Money Anxiety Index rose to 62.8, an increase of nearly 6 index points, and the unemployment rate rose to 4.3 percent, an increase of 0.3 percent—a clear indication of financial anxiety buildup. Fortunately, this was a short recession that officially ended in November 2001 without a lingering recovery tail.

Conversely, we were not as fortunate during the last recession, the Great Recession of 2007-2009, for which the transitional period of recovery is still going on at the writing of this book in mid-2013. Although the Great Recession officially ended in June 2009, we are still not out of the woods four years after the end of the recession. The Money Anxiety Index stood at 88.4 in June 2009, the official end of the Great Recession, and is at 90.3 in June of 2013—a slightly higher level of consumer financial anxiety despite four years of lingering recovery. The economic transitional period of recovery after the Great Recession is the longest on record in the past 50 years.

The Behavioralogy Matrix

Based on the evidence that consumer financial behavior reacts to present or anticipated economic conditions, we can now observe how consumers modify and orient their financial behavior to the four seasons of the economy: growth, decline and two transitional periods in between. Since the economic cycle repeats itself, and since consumers react to such economic changes in the same basic pattern, we can identify consumers' specific behavioral orientation during the different stages of the economic cycle.

Overall, I have observed six distinct behavioral orientations: three for saving and three for spending. These six behavioral orientations make up the behavioral matrix I am going to describe in detail. I titled each of the six behavioral orientations with a commonly used term rather than a "scientific" title because I believe that it's easier for us to associate our own behavior with those I am describing. I assure you that when you read the description, analysis and examples in each of these six behavioral orientations, you will be able to associate your own behavior with many if not all of them.

Remember that the following six behavioral orientations are not segmentation. These are not distinct groups of people, each behaving in a different manner. Rather, these are descriptions of six behavioral patterns that are shared by all or most of us regardless of our age, gender, income, education, or psychographic characteristics. Granted, some of us might follow these six behavioral orientations sooner than others, or to a greater degree than others, but overall we all have these behavioral orientations in common simply because we all share the same brain parts and functionality, which are at the core root of any human behavior.

I remember when I read "Think and Grow Rich" by Napoleon Hill for the first time many years ago; I was amazed by his description of the main human "emotions" as he defined them. Hill listed fear and greed as two of those emotions. I placed the definition of emotions in quotation marks not because I disagree with the content of his list and his brilliant

47

research, but rather because I think that fear and greed are not really emotions—rather they are instinctive and intellectual functions respectively because they emanate from different parts of the brain, not the emotional one.

According to Hill, among the "seven major negative emotions" are fear and greed. Hill was absolutely correct in placing fear at the top of the list because it is the strongest motivator of all. It was designed to be so because it ensures our survival. Of course, originally fear was designed to protect us physically; but in the context of this book, I am referring to fear from a financial aspect. At the time I read Hill's book for the first time I did not make the direct connection between fear and our instinctive brain functionality; I just took it at face value. Only later on, when I started conducting research on the topic of Behavioralogy, I made the connection between our brain functionality, our instinctive fear and our financial behavior.

Greed, which is also placed high on Hill's list, originates in our intellectual brain function. As we will see later in the section about the Behavioralogy matrix, greed comes into play mostly when the fear level subsides. In other words, as long as financial fear and anxiety are driving our financial decisions, greed is in the back seat. This is normal because in times of economic and financial anxiety, the first order of business is financial survival and preservation rather than spending and risk taking. The interaction between fear and greed plays a major role in Behavioralogy and in the six behavioral orientations I will outline shortly.

In the context of fear and greed, I also want to point out that the advertising industry is well aware of the role fear and greed play in our financial decision-making. Many advertisers use one or the other to make us buy their products, knowing that these two motivators are very strong and are likely to invoke a reaction from consumers. Think about commercials you see on TV or read in publications: how many of them use the term "safety" and "save"? Those commercials that stress safety are targeting the message to your fear factor, and those that feature savings, to your greed factor. One example that comes to mind is commercials for the car maker Volvo. Its commercials center around "drive safely", with images of children riding in the back seat of the car. This triggers your fears about your children's safety, which may result in your considering buying a Volvo next time you are in the market for a new car.

Below is the Behavioralogy Matrix, which outlines the six behavioral orientations and the behavioral patterns associated with each orientation. The column on the left contains the three behavioral orientations that impact savings, and the column on the right contains the three behavioral orientations impacting our decisions on spending. Notice that each column has three rows, corresponding to the economic seasons. The top row contains the behavioral orientation during high financial anxiety, which is typical during times of economic recessions. The bottom row is associated with economic growth and prosperity, and the middle row is associated with the two economic transitional periods in between recession and prosperity and vice versa.

CONSUMER SAVINGS	CONSUMER SPENDING
Mattress Money High financial anxiety Strong instinctive reaction Hoarding for survival	**Durable Diet** High financial anxiety Strong instinctive reaction Deferment of big spending
Power Play Indecisiveness due to uncertainty Power play between instinct and intellect Taking the safe way out	**Tiny Treats** Compensation for not buying big staff Emotional behavior takes over Feel good with little guilt
Rate Race Nothing can go wrong Intellect is fuelling greed The more the merrier	**Castle Craze** The bigger the better Real estate always appreciates My grass is the greenest

Consumer Savings

In a previous chapter I mentioned the importance of savings to the economy. No free-market economy can exist without savings, and neither can the banking system. Both depend on savings as means for leverage. Banks leverage deposits for lending. The extent of the leverage depends on the risk level of the bank's loan portfolio—the higher the risk, the greater the level of deposits needed to offset that loan. This was one of the issues with the collapse of the real-estate market during the Great Recession. Traditionally, mortgages are considered a less risky type of loan, which is one of the reasons the banking system was caught by surprise with a very high level of mortgage defaults. Since banks did not anticipate, and were not prepared for, such a high level of mortgage default, their liquidity level went below the minimum level required by the FDIC. Hence, the legislators and the government had to step in and bail out the banking system with tax-payer money.

I have no intention of expanding further on the particular events of the Great Recession, which are outside the scope of this book. Besides, these events have been already covered from every possible angle. The reason I bring up the connection to the Great Recession is to demonstrate the importance of savings to the economy and the banking system. Additionally I want to demonstrate the impact of taxation on consumer savings, which I will cover next.

Savings and Taxation

You probably remember the dramatic events of the fiscal cliff in December of 2012. Actually, we had warnings about the fiscal cliff throughout the year, but the heated discussion reached its crescendo during the last couple of weeks of 2012. The fiscal cliff had two aspects, a mandatory reduction in spending of about $85 billion, and expiration of the so called Bush tax cuts. I want to focus here on the expiration of the tax cuts because this is the part that could have impacted savings level and the economy the most.

On Friday, the 28th of December 2012, just three days before the expiration of the tax cuts (unless extended); I was contacted by the producer of the Kudlow Report on CNBC. The producer asked if I was willing to come on the show and be interviewed by Michelle Caruso-Cabrera on the possible impact of the tax cuts' expiration on consumers' savings. This was in response to an analysis I conducted showing that the expiration of the tax cuts in their entirety would reduce consumer savings by as much as 54.4 percent. I did appear on the CNBC show that afternoon, and presented the findings of the analysis.

I want to share the findings of this analysis with you because they clearly show how severe the impact of taxation can be on one of the pillars of the economy—consumer savings. The analysis shows that consumers increased their bank deposits nearly twice as much during the tax cuts period compared with the increase in deposits during times of higher taxes, and interest rates on deposits were not a factor. The looming expiration of the tax cuts on December 31, 2012 was likely to cause gradual decrease in the growth rate of bank deposits starting in 2013 and beyond. Fortunately, Congress voted to extend most of the tax cuts in the final hours before the expiration date, and thus prevented the adverse impact of higher taxes on consumer savings. Nevertheless, I think it is important to see the impact that higher taxes have on consumer savings and on the economy as a whole.

The analysis examined two time periods of nine years each, pre and post tax cuts. The first time period is from June 1992 to June 2001, a period prior to the enactment of the initial tax cuts measure, the Economic Growth and Tax Relief Reconciliation Act of 2001 (EGTRRA).. During this nine-year period, total deposits in FDIC insured institutions increased by $1.5 trillion, or 42 percent. However, during the nine years after the tax cut took effect, total deposits increased by $4.1 trillion, or 82 percent, which is nearly double the rate of growth compared to the first period. Interest rates on deposits were not a factor in the shift in deposit growth during these two time periods. During the pre tax-cuts period, the national average interest rate on deposits increased to a high of 3.35 percent in June of 2001, whereas during the post tax cuts period it decreased to 1.2 percent in June 2010.

The 82 percent growth rate during the post tax-cut period compared with 42 percent growth rate during the pre tax-cuts period already takes into account growth in population and inflation. However, it is possible that changing demographics and an increase in retiring baby boomers, who tend to save more conservatively, may have contributed to the growth rate in deposits during the tax-cut era. The Tax Policy Center estimated that an average household with an income of $75,000 could end up paying about $2,600 more in federal income taxes if the tax cuts expired. Again, this scenario was averted due to the extension of the tax cuts with some modifications.

Additionally, the analysis shows that the expiration of the tax cuts will reduce the amount of money each household has available to deposit in bank accounts from an average of 54.4 percent—from $4,782 to $2,182. A decrease of $2,600, which is the amount of added annual federal tax an average household will have to pay according to the estimates from the Tax Policy Center.

The total amount of consumer savings in bank accounts, excluding business and institutional accounts, increased from $3.8 trillion in December 2001 to $8.2 trillion in December of 2012. That's a total increase of $4.4 trillion or an average increase of $396 billion per year. When divided by 82.8 million U.S. households with banking relations, according to the FDIC, the average annual bank savings per household per year amounted thus far to $4,782. Once the expiration of the tax cuts takes effect, the average household will have only $2,182 available for savings in bank accounts, which is less than half of the average annual amount households deposited in bank accounts in the past 11 years. Below is the calculation based on data from the FDIC and US Census Bureau.

CATEGORY	FINDINGS
Total consumer (Retail) deposits on Dec, 2001 (FDIC)	$3,834,668,846,000
Total consumer (Retail) deposits on Dec, 2012 (FDIC)	$8,191,834,554,000
Total growth in consumer deposits	$4,357,165,708,000
Average growth in consumer deposits per year	$396,105,973,455
Total US households (US Census Bureau)	120,400,000
Total banking households (68.8 percent FDIC))	82,835,200
Average annual bank savings per year per household	$4,782
Average added federal tax per household without tax cuts	$2,600
Decrease in average annual bank savings after additional tax	$2,182
Percentage of decrease in funds available for saving	54.4%

Chapter Five

Behavioralogy of Consumer Savings

Mattress Money

Mattress Money is our most basic and oldest behavioral orientation. It stems from our instinctive brain—the first part of the brain to form—and is "responsible" for our survival. Of course, the original purpose of the instinctive brain had nothing to do with financial matters *per se*, but over time, as humans evolved and financial survival became critical, the instinctive brain started playing a role in our financial behavior.

Looking back at our ancestors, who lived in constant uncertainty regarding the elements, predatory animals and other threats to their physical survival, we can see why the instinctive brain evolved to become so dominant when we fear a looming danger. An example of such behavior would be reaction to (at that time) unexplained weather changes. If our ancestors noticed a change in cloud formation, temperature and other unexplained and misunderstood signs, they immediately hoarded food and wood in order to be prepared and ride out the storm. Keep in mind that our ancestors did not have the understanding we have today of weather patterns, and the ability to forecast storms and explain weather phenomena. For them, it was one big uncertainty about what's coming.

Our ancestors' instinctive reaction to uncertainty and the act of hoarding food and wood for survival is exactly the same instinctive reac-

tion we have today to economic and financial uncertainty, the only difference being that instead of hoarding food and wood, we do it with our
money. As we saw in the previous section, in the five years since the
Great Recession started, from 2007 to 2012, the amount of money people
saved in bank accounts increased by 30 percent compared to 9.7 percent
increase in saving during the five years prior to the Great Recession—a
three-fold increase in the amount of savings. This additional amount of
money consumers piled up in their savings accounts represents financial
hoarding.

But the instinctive behavior driving us to hoard money does not end
there. Saving money during times of economic and financial uncertainty
has a special form, which is at the core of the Mattress Money behavioral
orientation I will discuss next. Just as the name implies, Mattress Money
represents the tendency to keep the money under the mattress, where it is
readily available for use in case of a financial need such as loss of employment.

Saving money in the bank has two main forms: liquid and term. The
liquid form applies to accounts such as checking, savings and money
market, in which the money can be withdrawn at any time with no advanced notice to the bank or penalty in the form of a fee for early withdrawal. These three account types—checking, savings and money market—are therefore classified as liquid accounts because the money in these
accounts can be immediately liquidated into cash. Term accounts are certificates of deposits, CDs, which require a time commitment for leaving
the money in the account. For example, a one-year CD requires that you
leave the money in the account for one year in order to qualify for the
prevailing interest rate. Although you can withdraw the money from a
CD before the end of the term, it takes longer to do so; and it will cost
some money in the form of early withdrawal fees.

To demonstrate the behavioral orientation of Mattress Money, I compared two time periods. The first is the five years before the start of the
Great Recession, from December 2002 to December 2007, the official
start of the last recession. The second time period is the five years during

and post the Great Recession, from December 2007 to December 2012. Here again, I used bank account balances available from the FDIC.

As you can see from the graph below, during the first, pre-recession, time period, savings in both liquid accounts and term accounts increased. Balances in term accounts, which consist of certificates of deposits of varying terms from three months to five years, increased by 56.6 percent, from $1.66 trillion in December 2002 to $2.60 trillion in December 2007. This is a normal increase in balances of term accounts during times of economic growth and certainty. Similarly, during the same time period, December 2002 to December 2007, balances in liquid accounts, such as checking, savings and money market, increased by 40.3 percent, from $3.07 trillion to $4.31 trillion. This is also a normal growth rate for liquid accounts during times of economic and financial certainty.

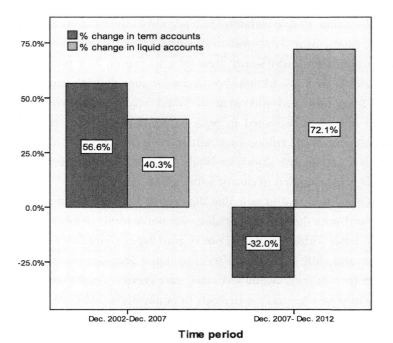

The most important aspect of the growth percentages in the pre-recession time period is that the percentage increase in balances of term accounts, 56.6 percent, is greater than the percentage growth rate in the balances of liquid accounts, 40.3 percent. A higher growth rate in the money people deposited in certificates of deposits, relative to liquid accounts, demonstrates their confidence in the economy because they are willing to lock the money up for a term, thus forgoing the ability to have instant access to the funds in case of need. This type of financial behavior indicates that people did not anticipate any urgent need for this money—such as a job loss as a result of higher unemployment due to declining economic activities.

Conversely, during the second time period, from December 2007 to December 2012, there was a major shift in the financial orientation of people who shifted money from term accounts to liquid accounts. We can clearly see in the graph that during the second time period, covering the Great Recession, people withdrew 32.0 percent of the balances they had in term accounts, from $2.60 trillion down to $1.77 trillion, and moved it over to liquid accounts, which grew by a whopping 72.1 percent, from $4.31 trillion to $7.43 trillion. We know for sure that the money withdrawn from term accounts went to liquid accounts because the total amount of money deposited in bank accounts during this time period increased from $8.42 trillion to $10.61 trillion; thus money did not leave the banks—it was just shifted to liquid accounts in order to be readily available for withdrawal in case of a financial emergency.

It is also important to note that the growth in liquid account balances during and post the Great Recession was not a result of higher interest rates. In other words, people did not rush to deposit more money in bank accounts and shift money from term to liquid accounts because the returns on their money, i.e. interest rates, were greater. On the contrary, the average interest rate paid on deposits in banks decreased during the second period, from 2.93 percent in December 2007 to 0.33 percent in December 2012—a decrease of 89 percent in the yield value of their money.

I wrote extensively on the phenomenon of Mattress Money and how consumers tend to hoard money in liquid form during times of extreme financial stress and anxiety. One article that captures this behavioral orientation very well was published by Cole Epley, staff reporter for the "Memphis Business Journal". In an article he wrote on April 27, 2007 titled: *"Banking consumers puzzling between security and profit"* he wrote: *"the balance of all CDs has dropped by nearly $700 billion nationally in the last five years. Dan Geller says the downward trend is ongoing, and that the proportion of total bank deposits comprising CDs fell from 31 percent of all bank deposits in January 2007 to just 18 percent at the end of 2011."*

Others commented on this phenomenon as well. In her article, "Americans Are Banking, Not Investing", Jonnelle Matte of "Smart-Money" wrote on January 30, 2012, *"Americans are largely yanking money out of stock funds and putting it into safer vehicles like bond funds and bank accounts. For instance, investors pulled nearly $29 billion out of equity funds in December while pouring roughly $10 billion into bond funds, according to data the Investment Company Institute released Monday. Meanwhile, monthly bank deposits, which include checking, savings and money-market and CDs, averaged $62 billion in 2011 through September—four times the average of 2010."*

As I indicated before, the tendency to hoard readily-available money is just like putting your money under the mattress, which is why I called this particular behavioral orientation Mattress Money. Since this behavioral orientation is inherent in our instinctive brain, we are very likely to default back to such financial behavior any time we feel economic or financial danger due to declining economic conditions. This is an important observation, because it allows businesses, banks and analysts to anticipate such a financial behavior in times of economic uncertainty. In the third section of this book, I will discuss the impact this and other behavioral orientations have on two of the most important business and financial models: price elasticity and risk elasticity. If you use any of these financial models in your business, make sure you get to that part of the book because it will change the way you view and use price elasticity of demand and risk elasticity under uncertainty.

Power Play

I mentioned earlier in the book that an economy has four major seasons, much like the climate system in most of the world. The two main economic seasons are, of course, economic growth and economic recession. From a pure macroeconomic prospective, if Gross National Product grows by about 3 percent quarter after quarter, the economy is in a growth mode. If, however, Gross National Product is negative two or more consecutive quarters, the economy is officially in a recession. But of course economies don't shift from growth to recession mode overnight; there is always a transitional period, or more precisely, two transitional periods. One period is the transition from growth to recession, i.e. decline, and the other transitional period from recession back to growth, i.e. recovery.

The Power Play behavioral orientation is basically the interaction between our instinctive brain and our intellectual brain during both transitional periods. The reason I named this behavioral orientation Power Play is that the interaction that takes place between these two parts of our brain is actually a power play between them—an internal struggle determining which one will take control of our financial behavior. Unlike the Mattress Money behavioral orientation, in which the instinctive brain is the clear "winner" and dominates our behavior to hoard and keep money handy in case of an immediate financial need, in the Power Play behavioral orientation there is no clear "winner" yet, which is what transitional periods are—an in-between stage until such time as either the intuitive brain dominates, as in the case of a recession, or the intellectual brain takes over, as in the case of economic growth..

The interaction, or the power play, between the instinctive brain and the intellectual brain is about how to respond to current and perceived economic conditions. Remember that the instinctive brain is like an early alarm system that alerts us to any looming danger, financial or otherwise. Thus, just as soon as the instinctive brain "feels" financial danger, in the form of friends who lost their jobs, neighbors who had difficulties selling their home etc., the self-preservation mechanism in the brain is turned on and the voice inside starts telling us to proceed with caution. At the same time, our intellectual brain is pulling us in the direction of higher returns on our money and greater financial risk because there aren't yet signs of economic danger—the stock market is sky high, home prices are through the roof and people are spending money like there is no tomorrow.

When it comes to savings, the power play between the instinctive brain and the intellectual brain goes something like this: the instinctive brain tells you to put more of your money in the bank even though the yield in the form of interest rates is not as much as you can get in the equity markets, but at least the principal is safe just in case you will need a financial cushion in the event of a job loss. Conversely, the intellectual brain is pulling you in the direction of putting the money in the equity market because the returns are so much greater and there is no looming danger to be concerned with.

The main "argument" of the instinctive brain in favor of hoarding and survival is the safety and security of the money. Unlike the equity markets, mutual funds and other forms of investments, bank and credit union deposits are insured up to $250,000. This means that the money you deposited in a bank or credit union, up to the defined limit, is insured, and no matter what, you will never lose the principal amount you deposited. Banks are insured by the Federal Deposit Insurance Corporation (FDIC), an independent agency of the United States government. The FDIC protects depositors in insured banks located in the United States against the loss of their deposits if an insured bank fails. Similarly, credit unions are regulated and insured by the National Credit Union Administration (NCUA), which like the FDIC regulates and insures credit unions' deposits.

Up until Congress passed the Emergency Economic Stabilization Act of 2008, the limit on deposit insurance was $100,000 per account holder per insured institution. The Emergency Economic Stabilization Act of 2008 temporarily increased the insurance limit to $250,000; and on July 21, 2010, President Barack Obama signed the Dodd-Frank Wall Street Reform and Consumer Protection Act into law, which, in part, permanently raised the current standard maximum deposit insurance amount (SMDIA) to $250,000. The FDIC insurance coverage limit applies per depositor, per insured depository institution for each account ownership category.

Again, the deposit insurance has a major role in the tendency of consumers to increase their bank deposits despite decreasing interest rates, because they know that the principal amount is always safe and secure. In contrast, during the Great Depression, when bank deposits were not yet insured, we witnessed a run on the banks as soon as economic conditions started to deteriorate. At that time, when a bank failed, any money held at that bank was lost. This did not occur during the Great Recession, and we did not experience a run on the money because of the FDIC and NCUA deposit insurance.

One of the main characteristics of the Power Play behavioral orientation is the tipping point. Tipping point occurs when consumers' sensitivity to interest rates relative to their savings changes from sensitive to insensitive, or in economic terms, from elastic to inelastic. In a "normal" scenario that follows the conventional model of price elasticity of demand, consumers gravitate towards the highest interest rates they can get on their deposits. This means that if a bank offers a higher interest rate on a CD than the interest rate a consumer currently receives, this consumer is likely to transfer the funds to the higher-interest bank at the end of the CD term. This type of relation between rates and money or balances is defined as sensitive or elastic because the amount of money in the bank will change based on the interest rates they offer to their customers.

Conversely, if consumers keep on piling money in their savings accounts without regard to the interest rates paid on such deposits, the relation between the interest rates and the money in the savings accounts is insensitive or inelastic. Here, again, it is important to note that the transition from elastic to inelastic is not sudden and does not occur overnight; it is a gradual process that takes place over time, which is why I call it a transitional period. Nevertheless, the point at which the transition occurs, the tipping point, is very obvious in the graph below, which shows the national average interest rates for deposits before and during the Great Recession based on a composite of rate data from the Federal Reserve.

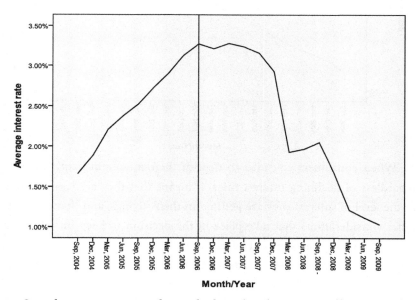

One does not even need to calculate the elasticity coefficient in this case (the percentage change in the amount of money deposited in banks divided by the percentage change in interest rates over the same time period). It is clear from the graph that from September 2004 until September 2006 the average interest rate paid on deposits was rising, and at the same time the total amount of deposits in banks was rising as well, as clearly indicated by the graph below. On the other hand, observe what happened after the tipping point of September 2006; the average interest rate on deposits was starting to decline, yet, the total amount of deposits in banks continued to increase.

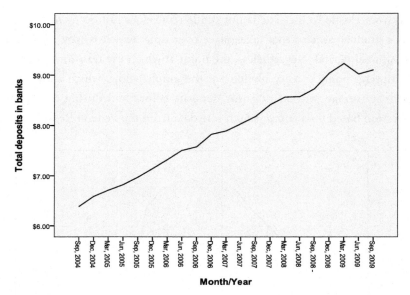

When consumers continue to deposit their money in bank accounts regardless of declining interest rates, it means that they are less sensitive to the level of interest they are getting on their savings, and that there are other considerations that take place in the decision to keep on piling up money in savings accounts. This is the period of inelasticity in the relation between interest rates and deposit balances.

It's important to distinguish between conventional price elasticity of demand and yield elasticity of demand. The conventional price elasticity of demand principle says that when price goes up, demand for that product or service will decrease, and vice versa. However, when it comes to bank deposits and interest rates, in other words yield elasticity, the rule is a mirror image of the conventional price elasticity of demand because higher interest rates are the equivalent of lower prices in consumer goods because both increase the consumer's buying power—lower prices leave more money in the consumer's pocket, and higher interest rates put more money there.

Earlier in this book I described how, in late 2006, I observed a discrepancy or a gap between the expressed level of consumer confidence, which is based on a subjective questionnaire, and the Money Anxiety Index, which is based on actual consumer financial behavior. This observation is directly related to the Power Play behavioral orientation I am describing here. Here is how it works. In response to the Thomson Reuters/University of Michigan Survey, consumers expressed an increase in their level of financial confidence from 93.6 index points in October 2006 to 96.9 in December of that year. On the other hand, the Money Anxiety Index started showing signs of higher financial anxiety starting in October 2006, when the index stood at 52.5, and increasing to 53.4 in December 2006. Thus, even though consumers reported high levels of financial confidence during the last three months of 2006, their actual financial behavior indicated higher financial anxiety. Keep in mind that the Money Anxiety Index is inversely structured to the consumer confidence index, which means that when the Money Anxiety Index goes up, it is similar to a decline in the consumer confidence index.

We can also see the connection between the decline in bank deposit interest rates, which started in September 2006, and the Money Anxiety Index showing an increased level of financial anxiety in October 2006. Clearly, consumers started seeing signs of financial danger as early as the last quarter of 2006 and acted accordingly by increasing their bank savings despite decreasing interest rates on such deposits. This type of shift in sensitivity to yields signals an entry into a transitional period from economic growth to an economic slowdown and possibly a recessionary period. As history shows, consumers were "right on the money" when they increased savings regardless of declining yields in the last quarter of 2006, because by December of 2007, we were officially in a recession.

Although the recession officially ended in June 2009, we are still in a transitional period as of the writing of this book in late 2013. This is the longest transitional period since the Great Depression. It has been nearly four years since the recession officially ended, and we are still not in a growth mode. More than that, as of this writing I do not see signs that we are entering a period of financial and economic growth. As a matter of fact, consumer financial anxiety is almost the same now as it was in June 2009, when the Great Recession officially ended. In June 2008, the Money

Anxiety Index stood at 88.4, and on June 2013, it stood at 86.2—a drop of only 2.2 index points in four years of recovery.

I mentioned earlier that during the many years of research I conducted in behavioral economics, I wrote many articles, analyses and papers on various aspects of this topic. Among them were a few on the record amount of consumer deposits during the last few years. One such article was published by CNN Money reporter Blake Ellis on August 25, 2012 titled: *Bank deposits hit record high of nearly $10 trillion*. The article describes that deposits in FDIC-insured banks climbed $343 billion in the first half of that year to an all-time high of $9.8 trillion despite meager interest rates, adding, *"Consumers are very fearful about the economy, and are fleeing to the safety and security of insured and liquid deposits," said Dan Geller."* Just as a side note, since the article was published in August 2012, deposits in banks continued to increase, despite historically low interest rates. By December of 2012, the total amount of consumer deposits in FDIC insured banks reached a high of $10.6 trillion.

Another article that features the record low interest rates we are experiencing during this economic transitional period was published in the "Wall Street Journal" on October 22, 2012 with the title "*Low Rates Pummel Banks*". In the article, reporter Dan Fitzpatrick describes how *"super-low U.S. interest rates are squeezing bank profits, complicating the industry's nascent recovery from the financial crisis."* The article continues describing the impact of historically low rates on consumers and banks: *"The prolonged low-interest rate environment is transforming the banking industry from savings and loans to service and loans," said Dan Geller. Deposit rates are already at their lowest levels since the 1950s; the five-year certificate of deposit dropped below 1 percent for the first time in mid-August and is now 0.93 percent."*

Another key article I wrote on the link between the historically high levels of consumer deposits in FDIC insured banks, despite historically low interest rates, was published in Banking Administration Institute (BAI), and describes the inelasticity of federally-insured bank deposits during a period of intense economic turmoil and public fear. *"An elastici-*

ty analysis of the relationship between deposits' annual percentage yield (APY) and balances, since the start of the recession in December of 2007, shows that bank deposits are among the most inelastic of commodities, even more so than gasoline, which is highly inelastic due to its absolute necessity. The latest figures on deposit balances and APY indicate that the long-term elasticity of deposits is 0.22 (highly inelastic) compared to 0.58 for gasoline. The closer the elasticity figure gets to 0.00, the less sensitive is demand to changes in price, or APY in the case of deposits."

The reason for this inelasticity is that there is simply no substitution for insured deposits as a "safe" place to park your money. Typically, demand for a product is more sensitive to price changes in the long run because consumers change their behavior over time by either reducing consumption or by finding a substitute product. For example, when gasoline prices go up and stay high for a long time, consumers tend to buy more fuel-efficient cars (hybrid or electric), drive less and/or use more public transportation. However, there is no other way to ensure that the principal amount is 100 percent safe, as in the case of insured deposits. All other options, such as equities, mutual funds, bonds and the like, carry some level of risk to the principal.

Clearly, the combination of fear, which is a major part of our instinctive-survival mechanism, and the lack of alternative safety for money in times of economic transition, pushed consumers to pile up money in bank deposits with complete disregard to interest rates.

Rate Race

The Rate Race behavioral orientation occurs at the tail end of the transitional period between a recession and the beginning of economic growth. When the economy starts to improve and grow, the demand for loans, for personal and business reasons, increases and financial institutions such as banks and credit unions need to attract more deposits, or as it is called, liquidity, in order to have money for loans. During times of economic growth, banks and credit unions increase interest rates on deposits in order to compete for the money they need as leverage for lending. The greater the need for deposits, or liquidity, the higher the interest rates on deposits will get.

Consumers are very receptive to such competition for their deposit money during times of economic growth mainly because their level of financial anxiety is lower; the instinctive part of the brain, which is focused on survival, does not play a major role in the decision process because fear and anxiety levels are low. Thus, the decision process during times of economic growth involves mostly the intellectual part of the brain, which is capable of making analytical calculations such as which interest rate is higher and which deposit or investment is more favorable.

We know that the intellectual function of the brain, or System 2, is involved in the decision-making process on interest rates because decisions on yields and returns requires analytical thinking. For example, when a consumer has to choose between locking $10,000 in a CD for a term of three years at a rate of 2 percent or for five years at a rate of 3 percent, the consumer has to calculate the marginal yield to make a determination whether a 1 percent additional interest per year is a worthwhile return for two more years of no access to the money.

In addition, since a growing economy promotes competition among financial institutions for consumer deposits, the consumer also has to use analytical capacity, or System 2, to shop for the best offers available and to choose the one that best fits his or her yield and time objectives. Since financial institutions compete for consumer deposits in the form of more favorable interest rates, it is very customary for financial institutions to offer "specials" during times of need for liquidity. These specials are in the form of higher interest rates, compared to their regular rates; but there are some limitations. One such limitation is time, meaning that special rates are a limited time offer and available only for, let's say, two months. These types of specials are the equivalent to a special sale in retail stores, such as a President's Day sale offering 50 percent off selected items.

An example of a deposit special would be a three-year CD that normally yields 2 percent, offered at 2.5 percent if the three-year CD is opened between January 15 and 31. Financial institutions use these specials to attract money that fits their liquidity needs for lending. For example, if demand for three-year auto loans increases at a particular bank, they are likely to offer a special for three-year CDs, which will provide them with the funding the bank needs to lend against the deposited money. As you can see, the need for liquidity is specific to each financial institution based on its lending needs.

The presence of deposit specials makes it even more challenging for consumers to make a decision because in addition to deciding which deposit product is right for them, consumers also have to decide which financial institution offers the best rates for the account they have in mind. This decision process, which involves the analytical function of the brain, or System 2, is the root cause of the Rate Race behavioral orientation.

Once the involvement of the instinctive function of the brain, in the form of financial fear and anxiety, is minimized, the intellectual function is in command of the decision-making process, and the Rate Race begins. Consumers are constantly exposed to advertising and promotions of financial institutions featuring their best interest rates on deposits, and the consumer has to sort through all this information to figure out which bank or credit union offers the best return on their money and most desirable terms of commitment. Clearly, the Rate Race behavioral orientation attracts deposits, as we can see from an actual example below.

To illustrate the Rate Race behavioral orientation, I selected the period between August 2003 and July 2007 because this was a time of economic growth, which is when the Rate Race is in full swing. August 2003 was the first month of rising interest rates on deposits after a long decline during the 2001 recession. August 2003 was the tipping point we discussed in the previous chapter. The average interest rate on deposits stood at 1.91 percent, and the Rate Race had begun. By July of 2007, which was the early stage of the Great Recession, the interest rate on deposits climbed up to

4.47 percent—an increase of 256 basis points or a relative increase of 134.6 percent in four years.

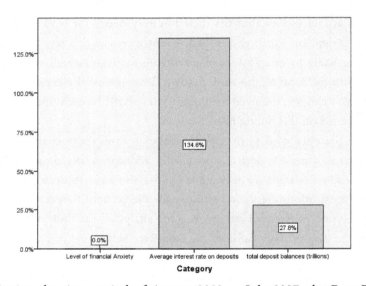

During the time period of August 2003 to July 2007, the Rate Race behavioral orientation had a great impact on the accumulation of deposits in banks. In August 2003, the total deposits balance in banks was $5.2 trillion, and it grew to $6.7 trillion by July of 2007—an increase of $1.5 trillion in four years, or a relative increase of 27.8 percent. Clearly, the Rate Race was very effective in attracting deposits to banks at a rate of $600 billion for each 1 percent increase in the average interest rates on deposits. Such a tremendous response to increasing interest rates on deposits had not occurred in the previous 20 years, which is as long as official governmental records on interest rates and deposit balances exist.

Remember that in most cases, higher interest rates are paid on longer term deposits, which means that many customers choose long-term certificate of deposits in order to qualify for higher interest rates and greater return on their money. Such behavior occurs only during the Rate Race orientation because consumers are making decisions using their intellectual brain function with very little or no intervention of the instinctive brain functions. We can clearly see from the graph above that financial fear and anxiety are not part of the Rate Race behavioral orientation because during the time period of the tremendous growth in interest rates and deposit balances, the level of financial anxiety, as measured by the Money Anxiety Index, was flat.

In this chapter I described the three behavioral orientations associated with consumer savings, which is one of the main pillars of the economy. In the next chapter, I will cover the three behavioral orientations associated with consumer spending—a critical factor in the economy because it makes up about 70 percent of Gross National Product, which is the total output of products and services in the U.S. Shortly you will see how the level of consumer financial anxiety can have a far reaching effect on specific industries and on the economy as a whole.

Chapter Six

Behavioralogy of Consumer Spending

Consumer spending—or as officially defined by economists, Personal Consumption Expenditures (PCE)—is a critical factor in the economy, especially in the U/S., where it makes up about 70 percent of total output of products and services. Consumer spending, or spending in short, is the fuel that enables the economy to grow. Since consumer spending constitutes such a large portion of GDP, it is easy to understand how critical spending is to maintaining and growing the economy. There are different models for measuring the multiplier effect of spending on the economy, but the principle is the same—every dollar that consumers spend impacts multiple aspects of the economy because by spending money on products or services, demand is created. This means that someone is getting paid to make the product or provide the service related to the purchased product, and this person is also a purchaser of other products and services. In short, when a consumer buys a new car, the money spent goes far beyond just the automaker that manufactured the car.

As we will soon see, there is no substitute for consumer spending. Government spending makes up only 19 percent of GDP, and clearly government cannot make up a substantial shortfall in consumer spending. Even with programs like quantitative easing (QE) and other stimulus programs, the impact cannot be a substitute for consumer spending. We witnessed such a case during the QE I and QE II programs after the Great

Recession. A few trillion dollars were pumped into the economy through these programs; but the impact was negligible. As of the writing of this book in late 2013, the economic recovery is still sluggish, and the Federal Reserve is reluctant to reduce the bond buying program or increase the Fed funds rate for that reason.

A look at the figures from the U.S. Department of Commerce on the fourth quarter 2012 GDP shows how sluggish the economic recovery is. The report by the U.S. Department of Commerce states: "Real gross domestic product—the output of goods and services produced by labor and property located in the United States—increased at an annual rate of 0.1 percent in the fourth quarter of 2012."

Keep in mind that one tenth of one percent GDP growth is practically flat GDP growth and is bordering on negative GDP growth. Recall that two consecutive quarters of negative GDP growth constitute a recession. So although we are not officially in a recessionary period, we are in a delicate transitional period that can easily turn into a recession if consumers hold back on current spending levels due to uncertainty about the prospects of economic recovery. The bottom line is that after five years since the start of the Great Recession, and after trillions of dollars in stimulus money, we are still in danger of falling back into a recession, and the economy does not have enough steam to pick up momentum. Why is it that after all this money that was artificially pumped into the economy we are not seeing the economy growing at a "normal" pace? The short answer is Behavioralogy, and next you will see how consumer financial anxiety plays a major role in economic boom and bust.

Spending, in and of itself, is not the solution to lack of economic growth. Rather, it's who spends and on what money is spent, which we will discuss next. The trillions in stimulus money that were spent by the government should have been enough to compensate for any shortfall in consumer spending, but as evident from the outcome, it did not. Artificial spending can't substitute for consumer spending without a change in the behavioral orientation of consumers. In other words, it's not about the numbers, or how much additional money is spent—it's the level of consumer financial anxiety that makes the difference. Let's look at the different behavioral orientations of consumer spending, and how they impact the economy.

Durable Diet

The Durable Diet behavioral orientation is the tendency of consumers to prolong the utility of durable products in times of high economic and financial anxiety. This behavioral orientation is rooted in the instinctive function of the brain, which is focused mostly on survival. In times of high financial anxiety, our instinctive function "directs" us to preserve what we have, especially high-ticket items, because of the uncertainty of future events—in our case, financial uncertainty. In other words, our instincts tell us to hold onto items of high replacement cost we have for as long as we can because we don't know if we will have the earning power to replenish the money spent if the economy is not doing well. Moreover, our instincts tell us to utilize our durable products for as long as we can because we might need money for other things which are more important and urgent, such as food, housing and clothing.

In order to illustrate the impact of the Durable Diet Behavioral Orientation on personal consumption and the economy, I compared two periods based on data provided by the Bureau of Economic Analysis. The first is the two-year period prior to the Great Recession, from September 2005 to September 2007, when the level of financial anxiety was relatively stable, and we had not officially entered the Great Recession. During this time period, from September 2005 to September 2007, total personal consumption increased by 10.4 percent - from $8,937 billion to $9,862 billion (thousands of billions is trillions, so $8,937 billion is $8.94 trillion.

Similar performance was also registered for durable goods, which increased by 9.95 percent in the two-year period prior to the Great Recession, from $1,104 billion to $1,210 billion. Nondurable goods increased by 7.97 percent, from $2,033 billion to $2,194 billion, and consumption of services increased by 11.34 percent, from $5,801 billion to $6,458 billion during the period of September 2005 to September 2007. Clearly, personal consumption increased across all major consumption categories at more or less the same pace.

Now let's look at what happened in a two-year period once we entered the Great Recession, when the Money Anxiety Index increased from 58.8 in September of 2007 to 93.6 September of 2009—an increase of 34.8 index points or 59 percent increase in the level of consumer financial anxiety. This is an enormous amount of added financial anxiety, which severely impacted consumer consumption and spending. Overall consumer consumption came to a halt during this two-year period. Consumer consumption stood at $9,862 billion in September of 2007, and by September 2009 it was almost at the same level of $9,872 billion—a meager increase of one tenth of one percent that does not even compensate for inflation.

But the real change occurred with consumption of durable goods, as illustrated in the graph below, which decreased by 16.3 percent during this two-year period, from $1,210 billion to $1,012 billion. This decrease is the essence of the Durable Diet behavioral orientation, which shows how consumers prolong the use of their durable and most expensive items during times of financial anxiety. Nondurable goods were practically flat during this time period—only 0.3 percent increase—and service consumption increased by 3.01 percent.

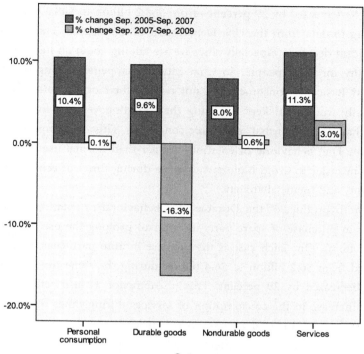

Category

Now that we have seen the big picture of how higher financial anxiety triggers an instinctive reaction of prolonging the use and utility of high-cost durable items, let's look at a specific example of a major durable item—automobiles. For most consumers, car purchase is the second largest expenditure after home buying. Moreover, an automobile is a necessity for most people because it is their means of transportation to and from work, school, child care etc. Thus, car buying for consumers who do not have the option of using public transportation, is necessary, and they would not be able to conduct normal life functions without it. Just for the record, the correlation coefficient between car sales and the Money Anxiety Index is -.358, which clearly shows how car sales go down when financial anxiety goes up and vice versa.

In the first year of the Great Recession, December 2007 to December 2008, while consumer financial anxiety was still very high, auto sales in the U.S. decreased by 29 percent—from $68.2 billion to $48.3 billion, according to data from the U.S. Department of Commerce. This is a very significant decrease, especially since we are talking about an item that is a necessity for most people. So what actually happened during this time period? Basically, consumers did not replace their cars as often as they normally would and kept on using their existing vehicles for a longer time than under "normal" economic conditions. This is a symptom of the Durable Diet behavioral orientation—longer-than-normal use of existing items in order to avoid high-cost expense during times of economic uncertainty and financial anxiety.

One byproduct of the Durable Diet behavioral orientation is an increase in purchase of spare parts in order to prolong the use of existing major items. One such case is the increase in auto-part sales, which increased from $6.2 billion to $6.4 billion during the same time that auto sales decreased by 29 percent. This phenomenon is also reflected in a slight increase in the consumption of services during times of economic uncertainty and financial anxiety. As we saw earlier in the chapter, during the two-year period from September 2007 to September 2009, while consumption of durable goods decreased by 16.3 percent, consumption of services actually increased by 3 percent. This basically means that more consumers opted to prolong the use of their cars, refrigerators, washing machines and other major appliances by either buying spare parts and fixing them by themselves, or having a service technician perform this service.

But the Durable Diet behavioral orientation goes beyond just automobiles; it encompasses many other durable items. For example, when we measure the correlation between the Money Anxiety Index, which measure the level of consumers' financial anxiety, and sales figures for furniture in the past 20 years, we see a negative correlation of -.364, which means that when the level of consumers' financial anxiety rises, sales of home furnishings go down. We can clearly see this negative relation in the sales figures. In January 2007, on the verge of the Great Recession, sales of furnishings amounted to $9.6 billion. By the end of the Great Recession, in June 2009, sales of furnishings went down to $7.2 billion—a decrease of $2.4 billion.

There is one more aspect to the Durable Diet behavioral orientation that makes it significant and a drag on the economy. Although every economic activity has a multiplier, meaning that a dollar spent triggers a chain of demand and production of related goods and services, durable goods have higher multipliers than nondurable goods or services because they are more complex and require involvement of more people and production capacity to produce them. For example, if you take the number of parts and production steps that go into an average automobile, it is much greater than the number of parts and production steps that go into the making of a pair of shoes. Therefore, from an economic perspective, more people benefit from every dollar spent on durable goods than from a dollar spent on a pair of shoes.

I want to go back to what I said earlier about the limitations of stimulus programs because, although the government and the Fed pumped money into the economy, this money did not have a great impact on the Behavioralogy of consumers. A case in point is the Durable Diet we just discussed. With all the trillions in stimulus money that was injected into the economy, consumers still halted their consumption during the two-year period from September 2007 to September 2009, and drastically decreased consumption of durable goods. So where did the stimulus money go? After all, some stimulus money went to public works projects, clean-energy projects and other major initiatives that employ many people. The answer is simple—consumers deposited much of the "extra" money in bank accounts in the form of Mattress Money, which is why consumer savings went up dramatically during the Great Recession.

Now you can see the connection between the two pillars of the economy—savings and spending. In times of economic uncertainty and high financial anxiety, consumers halt their spending and deposit more money in their bank accounts even if there is hardly any return on the money in the form of interest rates. This is the reason the Mattress Money behavioral orientation is the equivalent of Durable Diet on the consumption side. These two behavioral orientations go hand in hand during times of economic uncertainty and high financial anxiety.

You don't even need statistical analysis to figure this out—just think about your behavior during the Great Recession. Think about the two-year period from September 2007 to September 2009: did you buy a new car, new refrigerator, new big screen TV? For most people the answer is no, because Behavioralogy is shared by most people regardless of age, gender and even income. Chances are that most people followed the same behavioral orientation during this two-year period, avoided any non-urgent purchase of durable goods and increased their bank savings regardless of the meager interest rates.

Tiny Treats

The Tiny Treats behavioral orientation peaks during transitional times in the economy, mainly in the transition period from recessionary periods to growth periods. The main characteristic of the Tiny Treats behavioralogy is its function as a "comforting" act more than anything else. Keep in mind that during recessionary times, many consumers hold off on purchasing large-ticket items that are sometimes needed; but because of a high level of financial anxiety and economic uncertainty, consumers are delaying making decisions on such expensive items. Once a transitional period rolls by, meaning that the economy is not in the height of a recession, but not in a growth mode yet, consumers are starting to increase their spending a little—just enough to compensate themselves for all the times they could not afford even small treats for themselves.

Tiny Treats is an emotionally-based decision. It is a decision to make us feel good with little items that are not likely to deplete our savings account; yet they can make us feel better. Examples of Tiny Treats are items or services for health and personal care. Let's take a look at actual figures of retail sales of health and personal care items, reported by the U.S. Department of Commerce, for two economic periods of two years each. The first time period is during recessionary time, from January 2008 to January 2010, and the second time period is during a recovery or transitional time from January of 2010 to January 2012.

In the graph below, you can see that during the recessionary period of January 2008 to January 2010, total sales of health and personal care items increased by about 5 percent. Conversely, during the two-year period of recovery or transitional time from January 2010 to January 2012, the increase in sales of health and personal items in retail stores increased dramatically to 8.34 percent. I purposely selected two consecutive time periods in order to eliminate any possibility that the growth in sales of health and personal care items was a result of a major population growth or other factors that could have impacted retail sales of health and personal care items in such a dramatic way. Clearly, the only change during the combined four-year time span was that we transitioned from a recessionary period to a transitional or recovery period.

I am sure that each of us has our favorite Tiny Treats—those things with which we treat ourselves when we want to compensate ourselves for an effort we did or a sacrifice we made. Of course, in good economic times, we treat ourselves with much more lavish rewards such as an overseas trip or expensive jewelry. But in times of high or moderate economic uncertainty and financial anxiety, we lower the bar to more affordable items such as a beauty-care item or a massage after a long and stressful week at work.

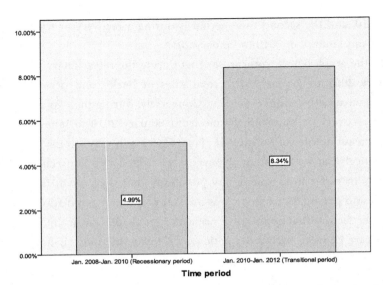

Here is an anecdotal example of how the Tiny Treats behavioral orientation manifests itself in real life. The other day I was talking to my friend Judy about the book I am writing. I described to her some of the interesting findings from my analysis of Behavioralogy. At that time, in mid-2013, we were in a transitional period from the Great Recession to a slow and gradual recovery, and I described to Judy the unique behavior of Tiny Treats during such transitional periods in the economy. Judy stopped me abruptly and said "Wow, this is exactly what my coworker is doing—now I understand why." I was very curious about her observation and asked her to describe the behavior. It turns out that after the Great Recession, the husband of Judy's coworker lost his job, and they had to start cutting back on expenses. They had to take their kids out of private school and eliminate all non-essential spending. Nevertheless, according to Judy, the one thing her coworker did not give up was her weekly nail treatment at a cost of about $30. This is a classic example of Tiny Treats Behavioralogy—allowing yourself a small personal treat that makes you feel good about giving up all the other things you can no longer afford during transitional economic times.

The message to business and financial people is to constantly be tuned in to the behavioral orientation of consumers, as reflected by the Money

Anxiety Index, in order to detect trends and shifts in consumers' financial behavior. The advantage of such an "early detection" system is that businesses can adjust inventories and marketing and advertising campaigns to be in sync with the shift of consumers' preference for goods and services. Similarly, investors should monitor the level of consumers' financial anxiety because a shift in consumer demand can have an immediate and drastic impact on the financial performance and profitability of traded companies.

Castle Craze

As soon as the economy improves and starts to show meaningful signs of growth, consumers return to their favorite "sport"—bigger and better homes. The Castle Craze behavioralogy is about consumer fascination with bigger, better and nicer homes the moment they feel that the economic storm is over. Clearly, real estate, specifically the primary residence property, is very appealing—not just from a practical perspective of a place to live and for investment reasons, but also as a statement of status and achievement.

By now many of us are very familiar with the real estate boom and bust that occurred during the early to late 2000s. So I am going to skip the whole story about who did what and why in regards of mortgages, securitizations and everything else that is related to the rise and fall of the real estate market in the last economic cycle. Instead, I would like to focus on the behavioral aspect of the period prior to the collapse of the real estate market to demonstrate the Castle Craze behavioralogy orientation.

The main factor in the Castle Craze behavioral orientation is the amount of money consumers spend on their homes, in terms of building supplies and gardening equipment during good economic times, compared to other types of spending. To demonstrate the Castle Craze behavioral orientation, I selected the four-year period prior to the actual start of the Great Recession, from February 2003 to March 2007. Keep in mind that although the official start date of the Great Recession was December of 2007, the actual decline in the economy started about six months prior to that because it takes two consecutive quarters of negative GDP to declare an official recession. Thus, the actual decline in economic activities started in the second quarter of 2007.

In the graph below, I compared the percentage increase in total retail sales between February 2005 and March of 2007 with the percentage increase in building and gardening supplies during the same time period. I am sure you are familiar with the phrase "high tide lifts all ships," which is only half true in this case. In this case, the robust economy during the early and mid-2000s lifted the sales of building and gardening supplies much higher than it did other categories of retail sales. While total retail sales during this four-year period increased by a substantial 26.4 percent, the percentage increase in building and gardening suppliers was 37.9 percent—a difference of 11.5 percent.

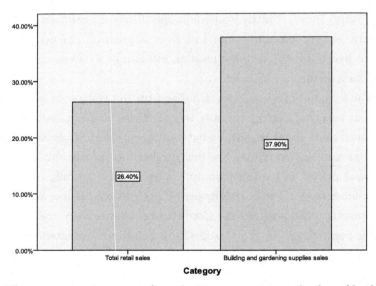

The enormous increase of nearly 38 percent in retail sales of building and gardening supplies, compared to other retail areas, is a clear indication of consumers' infatuation with building, improving and enhancing their homes during periods of economic growth and low levels of financial anxiety. Needless to say, this craze died right after the economy started declining in mid-2007, and although the real estate market is showing some signs of recovery at this time, mid 2013, it is very far from where it was during the growth years prior to the Great Recession.

It is also important to indicate that the growth figures in sales of building and gardening supplies are retail figures only and do not include large wholesale purchases of building materials used in the development of large housing and commercial complexes. Thus, the increase in retail sales of building and gardening supplies during the four-year span we discussed earlier accounts for purchase by individual consumers and small contractors working mostly on smaller building or renovating projects.

Will we see another cycle of Castle Craze behavioral orientation down the road? Yes, of course. This was not the first, nor is it the last, economic cycle we are going to experience, and once the economy starts growing again, we will witness the same type of behavioral orientation repeating itself. Why? Because, as we discussed earlier in the book, human nature never changes, only circumstances do. Just as soon as the level of financial anxiety decreases and consumers feel more confident about the economy, they will be thrown back to building and remodeling their castle that was "neglected" in the last few years since the beginning of the Great Recession.

The Castle Craze behavioral orientation is a very important indicator for almost any type of business, retail and financial. The reason is that real estate has the highest economic multiplier among all other products and services. This means that when the real estate market starts growing, it impacts a very large number of other products and services associated with homes and gardens such as building materials, furnishings, appliances, gardening equipment and many other products and services related to building and maintaining homes.

The link between a lower level of financial anxiety and a higher level of building materials is very good news for the financial industry, because when the Money Anxiety Index starts declining, it means that consumers will start seeking mortgages for new homes, refinancing of existing mortgages, or home equity lines of credit or loans to finance the improvements they want to make in their homes. Thus, financial and banking professionals should keep a close eye on the Money Anxiety Index for signs of consistent decline in the level of consumers' financial anxiety, which is going to trigger the Castle Craze behavioral orientation.

All in all, when the Castle Craze behavioral orientation is taking place, the economy is going to greatly benefit from the financial boost it provides to many industries. As long as the financing side of the Castle Craze is done responsibly, Castle Craze behavioral orientation is highly desirable and a major contributor to economic growth and prosperity. In the next section of the book, part three, I am going to provide specific, practical and simple methods of gauging the economic impact of financial anxiety on the retail and financial industries.

Specifically, I am going to provide an enhanced method of determining the price elasticity of demand for any product or service that will improve any business person's ability to determine the optimal price and inventory level based on consumers' level of financial anxiety. For financial practitioners and researchers, I will provide an enhanced model of risk-based decisions that increases the accuracy of the amount of profit investors are willing to gain at various levels of risk.

Part Three

Behavioralogy in Decision Making

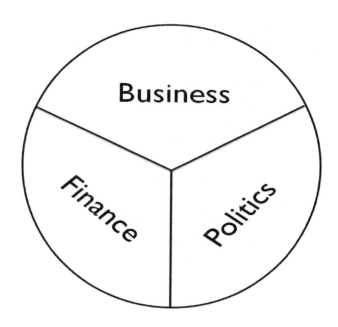

Financial anxiety is a major factor in business, finance and political decisions.

Now that we have covered the principles and types of financial behavior, it's time to explore the applicability of consumer financial behavior in business decisions. Regardless of our occupation or field of interest, we often have to make decisions that will impact us either positively or negatively. By now we have seen that our financial behavior is impacted by our level of money anxiety. The purpose of this section is to take this concept one step farther and explore how and to what degree the level of financial anxiety impacts two very common and useful financial models—price elasticity of demand, and risk-based decisions.

In this section, I will incorporate the principles of behavioralogy with price elasticity of demand and risk-based decisions, so that you will be able to use them in your business or occupation. Whether you work in the financial sphere or are a banker, retailer, business person, psychologist, economist or just someone who wants to understand how consumer financial behavior impacts some of the current analytical models, this section of the book will be very helpful to you.

Any business that deals with consumers, regardless of type and size of the enterprise, is exposed and subject to the principles of behavioralogy; and thus it must incorporate the level of consumer financial anxiety into its practice. The notion that consumers of the same demographic or psychographic segment always behave in a similar pattern is outdated and erroneous. As we have seen in the chapter on segmentation vs. orientation, consumers shift their financial behavior during various levels of money anxiety even if their demographic and psychographic segment has not changed.

Distinguishing between consumer segmentation and orientation is a critical point in understanding the role that behavioralogy plays in financial decisions and financial outcome. Consumers' demographic and psychographic segmentations are static in nature, meaning that their affiliation with a certain segment does not fluctuate based on macro-economic conditions. As we saw earlier, that is not the case in their real life behavior—the savings and spending patterns of all demographic and psychographic segments changed based on the level of financial anxiety. Therefore, financial anxiety is a critical factor in shaping the financial behavior of consumers, and must be incorporated into financial models and decision-making processes.

There are many business and financial applications to behavioralogy; however, in this part of the book I will discuss and demonstrate the need for incorporating consumers' financial anxiety into the use of price elasticity of demand and risk-based decisions. These two financial models are central to any type of business operating in a free-market environment. Determining the price elasticity of demand, which I will refer to as simply "elasticity", is important to any type of business because it provides the foundation for establishing the optimal price for the product or service and allows projection of demand, inventories and profitability. Similarly, making decisions between two choices that carry an equal chance of financial gain or loss is a common practice in business. Thus, the ability to establish an amount of gain needed to offset a probable financial risk of loss is helpful because it will prevent us from making choices that will not provide us with the desired financial or emotional gain.

In chapter seven, I will demonstrate why the conventional model of price elasticity of demand is flawed, and how we can correct this flaw with a simple solution. My goal is to provide you with a simple, practical and easy to use method to improve your business and financial decisions without the need to use sophisticated software programs or countless hours of calculations—I already did it for you in my many years of research and analysis. Once you read the chapter on the flaws of conventional elasticity, you will immediately be able to apply the new and improved model to your own scenario, and be able to figure out the real elasticity of your products or services.

In chapter eight, I will cover another important aspect of business and financial practices: making decisions under risk. Here, too, the goal is to provide you with a simple, practical and easy way to calculate the desired financial gain needed to offset the risk of financial loss based on the two current models of calculating financial risk—the Expected Utility Theory and Prospect Theory. There are other theoretical models for risk-based decisions, but these two are the prevailing theories at this time. The goal of chapter eight is to show you how incorporating the level of consumer financial anxiety into the calculation makes the outcome much more realistic and reliable. As a result, you will be able to improve the assessment of your financial decisions on gain and loss.

Finally, in chapter nine, I will provide a prospective on the link between financial anxiety and politics—specifically, presidential elections. Chapter nine provides a validation to the age-old saying that people vote with their wallets and purses. You will see how in the last 50 years, the political fate of each incumbent president running for re-election was determined by the level of consumer financial anxiety.

Chapter Seven

Financial Anxiety and Price Elasticity

Price Elasticity of Demand

Price elasticity, or by its full name, price elasticity of demand, has been around since 1890, when Alfred Marshall introduced "elasticity of demand" in his book *Principles of Economics*. Marshall started writing the *Principles of Economics* in 1881. His plan for the work gradually extended to a two-volume compilation on the whole of economic thought, which included the first volume (published in 1890) and a second volume, which was to address foreign trade, money, trade fluctuations, taxation, and collectivism, but was never published at all. Over the next two decades he worked to complete his second volume of the *Principles of Economics*, but never finished it.

The concept of determining price elasticity by measuring the percentage change in demand as a function of percentage change in price is limited, and current pricing models that are used to calculate price elasticity based solely on this formula lack a major component—the level of consumer financial anxiety, or Behavioralogy. In the case of consumer goods, price elasticity of demand (a.k.a PED or E_d) is used to show the responsiveness, or elasticity, of the quantity demanded of a good or service to a change in its price. It gives the percentage change in quantity demanded in response to a one percent change in price. For example, if in January of a particular year 1,000 units of a product were sold nationally, and in December of the same year the number of units sold increased to 1,100 units, than the change in demand is 100 units or 10 percent. If during the same time period, the price per unit changed from $10 in January to $15 in December, the increase in price is $5 or 50 percent. A simple division of the percentage increase in demand, 10 percent, by the percentage increase in price, 50 percent, provides us with the conventional elasticity of demand. Therefore, the elasticity coefficient of this product is 0.2, which means that this product is inelastic, and demand for this particular product is not sensitive to changes in price.

The rules for determining if a product or service's calculated elasticity is elastic or inelastic are very simple and straight forward. The three rules below provide the essence of determining the conventional price elasticity of demand. It's also important to keep in mind a couple of side notes. The first is that the price elasticity coefficient is typically a negative number. However, for the purpose of figuring out price elasticity we ignore the minus sign and all elasticity coefficients are presented in their absolute form. The other issue that deserves noting is that the conventional price elasticity of demand model, which we are discussing here, is also called "own price elasticity of demand". The reason for that is that the measurement of elasticity is based on changes in the product or service's own price and demand and no other factors are taken into consideration. This, by the way, is the root cause of the main flaw in the conventional price elasticity model, which I will discuss shortly. But first, here are the three basic elasticity rules:

- If the calculated price elasticity of demand is greater than 1.0, then demand is price elastic, which means that demand is sensitive to change in price.
- If the calculated price elasticity of demand is equal to 1.0, then demand is unit elastic, which means that demand will change exactly in the same percentage of the price change.

- If the calculated price elasticity of demand is less than 1.0, then demand is price inelastic, which means that demand is not sensitive to price changes.

Over the years, modifications were made to the conventional elasticity model to address various flaws, but none of these modifications addressed the issue of the impact of consumers' financial behavior on the relations between price and demand. Some of the enhancements to the conventional model were the point-price elasticity model, which calculates the elasticity for an infinitesimal change in price and quantity at any given point on the demand curve. Recall that the conventional elasticity model measures the percentage change in quantity demanded in response to percent change in price between two points in time. However, the percentage difference of either price or demand can vary even if the values themselves are the same just that in one case they are increasing and in another case they are decreasing. For example, if quantity demanded increases from 20 units to 30 units, the percentage change in demand is .50 - i.e., (30 − 20) ÷ 20, which comes out to 50 percent. However, if quantity demanded decreases from 30 units to 20 units, the percentage change is .33 - i.e., (30− 20) ÷ 30=33.3 percent. Another attempt to improve the validity of the conventional elasticity model is through the arc elasticity, or midpoints formula, which uses the average price and average quantity as the coordinates of the midpoint of the straight line between the two given points.

When looking at the list of determinants that may impact the degree of elasticity, it is clear that all of them are indicators and none are factors. In statistical terms, indicators are variables that can be observed and measured, whereas factors are latent variables that can't be directly observed or measured. The only way to measure a factor is through its impact on the dependent variables. These determinants include availability of substitution, income level and duration of goods' availability. None of these variables represent factors such as consumer financial anxiety, which plays a major role in consumers' decision to buy products or services, and for how much, during varying economic times.

One more thing about price elasticity as it relates to demand. Demand of any kind, be it demand for financial services or consumer goods, is greatly impacted by the level of necessity for that product or service, and by the availability of substitution. Generally speaking, the higher the necessity of a product or service, the greater the likelihood of inelasticity. Similarly, the absence of substitution or alternative products or services increases the likelihood of inelasticity. These rules are very logical because if a product or service is absolutely necessary to our survival and livelihood, and if we can't find an alternative or substitution that provides similar attributes, we are more likely to pay higher price to obtain these products or services. Let's look at the role of necessity in elasticity.

Necessity and Elasticity

I am going to use an example from the banking industry because the data is readily available on the Federal Deposits Insurance Company (FDIC) website. The FDIC, which is a governmental agency, provides weekly updates on the national average interest rates on various bank deposits, such as checking, savings, money market and certificates of deposit, as well as quarterly updates on the total balances for all deposits types. This information is available to the public.

Bank deposits are among the most inelastic commodities, sometimes even more than gasoline, which is highly inelastic due to its absolute necessity. The latest figures on deposit balances and interest rates indicate that long-term elasticity of deposits is 0.22 (highly inelastic) compared to 0.58 long-term elasticity for gasoline. The closer the elasticity figure is to 0.00, the less sensitive demand is to changes in price, or yield in the case of deposits. Short term (1 year or less) elasticity for deposits is at par with gasoline, 0.28 and 0.26 respectively, as illustrated in the graph below.

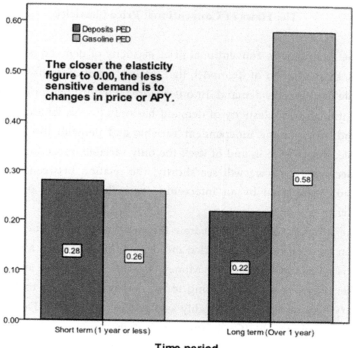

The reason deposits are more inelastic in the long term than gasoline is that there is no alternative to insured deposits. Typically, demand is more sensitive to price changes in the long run because over time consumers change their behavior by either reducing consumption or finding an alternative. When gasoline prices go up and stay high for a long time, consumers tend to buy more fuel efficient cars (hybrid or electric), drive less and/or use more public transportation. However, in the case of deposits, there is no alternative because there is no other way to ensure that the principal amount is 100 percent insured by the government up to the limit of $250,000 per account holder. All other options, such as equities, mutual funds, municipal bonds and the like, carry some level of risk to the principal.

DAN GELLER, PH.D.

The Flaws of Conventional Price Elasticity

The main flaw in conventional price elasticity of demand is that it assumes, by the design of its model, that price—in and of itself—is the sole variable that impacts demand. In other words, the formula for calculating conventional price elasticity of demand has only two variables, price and demand; price as the independent variable and demand the dependent variable. But is price in and of itself the only variable impacting demand? Not necessarily. As we will see shortly, the relation between price and demand is impacted by an intervening variable—the level of financial anxiety.

The simplest way to demonstrate the role consumer financial anxiety plays in the relation between price and demand is to conduct a regression analysis with and without the Money Anxiety Index as an intervening variable. Here, again, I am going to use an example from the banking industry because the data is readily available on the Federal Deposits Insurance Company (FDIC) website. One of the main uses of regression analysis is the ability to measure the explainable relations between two variables. In other words, how much, in percentage, does the independent variable explain changes in the dependent variable? In our case, we want to know the percentage of the impact that the national average interest rate on deposit has on deposit balances in domestic bank accounts. Or put differently, when interest rates on bank accounts change, what percentage of the change in the balances of these accounts can be attributed directly to the change in interest rates?

The regression analysis on the FDIC data from May 2009, when the FDIC fist started publishing national average interest rates, to June 2013, shows that 82.5 percent (R square = .825) of the changes in the balances of domestic bank accounts are impacted by the changes in interest rates. But what about the remaining 17.5 percent (100 percent minus 82.5 percent)? To find out, we need to run another regression analysis, this time including the Money Anxiety Index as an additional independent variable. The results show that the level of consumer financial anxiety adds 8

96

percent to the explainable relation between interest rates and demand for bank deposits. Together, interest rates and the Money Anxiety Index explain 90.5 percent of the changes in bank deposits. Clearly, the level of consumer financial anxiety plays a role in the relation between price and demand, and should be incorporated into any type of elasticity calculation.

Measuring Real Price Elasticity of Demand

Now let's look at how we can improve the conventional elasticity model by incorporating the element of consumer financial anxiety into the calculation. Recall that the calculation of the conventional price elasticity is done by dividing the percentage change in demand by the percentage change in price over a given time period—usually one year for short term elasticity, and three years for long-term elasticity. To calculate conventional price elasticity we follow this formula:

Price Elasticity of Demand = % change in demand divided by % change in price

Example: 10 percent change in demand divided by 5 percent change in price = 2.0 (Elastic)

From here on, converting the conventional price elasticity to real elasticity, which accounts for the level of consumer financial anxiety, is simple and straightforward. The process involves only two simple steps. First we find out the Money Anxiety Factor, by dividing the current Money Anxiety Index level by the historical average of the Money Anxiety Index. The reason we divide the current money anxiety level by the average money anxiety level is to find out whether the current anxiety level is above or below the historical average. For example, in July of 2013, the Money Anxiety Index stood at 88.3, and the 50-year average, a.k.a. historical average, of the Money Anxiety Index is 70.7. Therefore, the calculation of the Money Anxiety Factor is as follows:

Money Anxiety Factor = current anxiety level (88.3) divided by historical average (77.7) = 1.25

Second, we multiply the Money Anxiety Factor by the conventional elasticity—that's all there is to it. We have now converted the conventional elasticity coefficient into a real elasticity coefficient that takes into consideration the level of consumer financial anxiety and increases the accuracy and reliability of the price elasticity reading. Now let's incorporate the Money Anxiety Factor into an example of conventional elasticity:

Real elasticity = Conventional elasticity (1.2) times Money Anxiety Factor (1.25) = 1.5 (Inelastic)

In the example above, the Money Anxiety Factor of 1.25 increased the level of elasticity from 1.2 to 1.5, which means that under the current relatively higher level of consumer financial anxiety, demand for the product in the example above is even more sensitive to fluctuation in price. Conversely, if the level of consumer financial anxiety was lower than the historical average, then the sensitivity of the demand to price changes would have been lower. Let's look at a case where the Money Anxiety Factor is 0.8, which means that the current level of consumer financial anxiety is lower than the historical average. If we multiply the conventional elasticity in the above example—1.2—by the Money Anxiety Factor of 0.8, the coefficient is .96, which means that the real elasticity of this product is inelastic and not elastic as the conventional elasticity indicates.

Real elasticity = Conventional elasticity (1.2) times Money Anxiety Factor (0.8) = 0.96 (Elastic)

The logic behind real elasticity is that a higher level of financial anxiety increases the sensitivity of demand to price changes because consumers are less likely to spend during times of financial stress and economic uncertainty. Conversely, when the level of consumer financial anxiety is lower than the historical average, the sensitivity of demand to price changes is likely to be lower because consumers are more likely to spend money during periods of lower level of financial anxiety and when economic conditions are favorable.

Now that we have explored the principle of real elasticity, let's see how it works in actual cases of conventional elasticity of common products. The conventional elasticity of alcoholic beverages makes a good example because some are elastic and some are inelastic, so the comparison will provide us with an opportunity to see how their conventional elasticity changes at varying levels of consumer financial anxiety.

According to a study by Frank J. Chaloupka et al (2002), the elasticity of alcoholic beverages is as follows:

Alcoholic beverages (US)

- 0.7 for Beer (inelastic) – Demand is not sensitive to price changes
- 1.0 for Wine (unit elastic) – Demand is neutral to price changes
- 1.5 for Spirits (elastic) – Demand is sensitive to price changes

Now let's see what happens when we expose these conventional elasticity coefficients to the level of consumer financial anxiety during two levels of money anxiety—one higher than the historical average, and one lower. The reason I am choosing to demonstrate the impact of consumer financial anxiety on conventional elasticity over two different levels of financial anxiety (high and low) is to stress the point that elasticity is dynamic rather than static. This means that the same product or service can have a different elasticity coefficient depending on the level of consumer financial anxiety rather than just one fixed level of elasticity at any time. Moreover, in this actual case, I will show how demand for a product can shift from inelastic to elastic based on the change in the level of consumer financial anxiety.

For example, let's say that we want to measure the real elasticity of beer in July of 2013, which is a time of relatively high financial anxiety. First we calculate the Money Anxiety Factor for July of 2013 by dividing the July Money Anxiety Index of 90.3 by the historical average of the Money Anxiety Index, which is 70.7. The outcome is 1.3, which basically means that as of the writing of this book, consumer financial anxiety is greater than the historical average. If the Money Anxiety Factor is greater than 1.0, which is the case in mid-2013, we can expect a higher level of sensitivity to prices of most products and services. If the Money Anxiety Factor is lower than 1.0, it means that the level of consumer financial anxiety is lower than the historical average, and thus consumers are likely to be less sensitive to price changes of products and services. Finally, if the Money Anxiety Factor is equal to 1.0, then the real elasticity is equal to the conventional elasticity.

Let's return to the example of conventional elasticity of alcoholic beverages to examine how the price sensitivity changes during varying times of consumer financial anxiety. If we multiply the conventional elasticity of beer, which is 0.7 by the Money Anxiety Factor during times of very high financial anxiety, as was the case during the recession of the early 1980s, when the Money Anxiety Index reached a high of 135.0, we arrive at a Money Anxiety Factor of 1.9 (135/70.7). Therefore, the real elasticity of beer in November of 1982 was 1.9—highly elastic—rather than the reported conventional elasticity of 0.7, which is inelastic. This means that during the recession of the early 1980s, when the Money Anxiety Index reached as high as 135, consumers of beer were much more sensitive to the price of beer compared to times of lesser financial anxiety. Thus, although consumers of beer are generally considered insensitive to price changes, in reality they are very sensitive to price changes during times of extremely high levels of financial anxiety.

If you are wondering what the real elasticity of beer is at the time of the writing of this book in mid-2013, the answer is nearly unit elastic. This means that an increase in price of beer will result in the same percentage decrease in demand for beer. Here are the numbers—Money Anxiety Factor as of June 2013 is 1.3 (90.3/70.7) times the conventional elasticity of beer at 0.7 equals 0.91, which is still inelastic but getting closer to being unit elastic. So as of now, demand for beer is likely to change at almost the same percentage as the changes in price. However, if the level of consumer financial anxiety increases in the future, beer consumption would be likely to decrease if the prices were to increase.

We are all familiar with the generally accepted notion that during periods of hard economic times, consumption of alcohol goes up. This is only partly true; here is why. First, various types of alcoholic beverages, such as beer, wine and spirits, have different price sensitivities; and as we will see shortly, wine and spirits are very elastic and sensitive to higher prices, especially during times of high financial anxiety. This means that during times of high financial anxiety, consumption of alcohol might go up overall, but the consumption of alcohol per consumer declines. Let me explain that. If overall consumption of alcohol is up during periods of hard economic times, it means that more people are consuming alcohol, but not necessarily that individual consumers are drinking more alcohol.

Now that we saw how high financial anxiety increases consumers' price sensitivity to beer prices, let's examine the real elasticity of wine and spirits. The conventional elasticity of wine is 1.0, which is unit elastic. This means that the same percentage increase in price will be reflected in the decrease in demand, and vice versa. So if the price of wine went up 10 percent in a given time period, the decrease in demand is also expected to be 10 percent. Now let's subject wine elasticity to a high level of consumer financial anxiety of 135, which we experienced in the recession of the early 1980s. Here, again, we simply multiply 1.0 (wine conventional elasticity) by 1.9, which is the Money Anxiety Factor, to come up with real elasticity of 1.9 (1.0X1.9) for wine during times of high financial anxiety. This is an example of how one type of alcohol, wine, can turn from unit elastic to elastic during times of high level of consumer financial anxiety.

A similar scenario occurs with spirits, which have a conventional elasticity of 1.5, meaning that consumers of spirits are sensitive to increase in prices and are very likely to buy less spirits, or substitute less expensive alcoholic beverages, when prices of spirits go up. Once we calculate the real elasticity of spirits, which is highly elastic at 2.9 (1.5 X 1.9), we understand why in times of high financial anxiety, consumers of spirits are even more likely to buy less spirits or substitute with cheaper types of alcoholic beverages. This is also a good example of substitution. Most people who consume alcoholic beverages do not just stop drinking during stressful economic times—they just replace higher-cost alcoholic beverages with lower cost alcoholic beverages.

On the other hand, during times of low financial anxiety, the party goes on, with premium labels, because even wine and spirits become less sensitive to price changes. Wine, which has a conventional elasticity of 1.0, turns into an inelastic product during times of low financial anxiety. Similarly, even spirits, which have a conventional elasticity of 1.5, meaning elastic, turns into an inelastic product when the Money Anxiety Factor reaches the level of 0.65.

So what does it all mean? Simply put, during times of high financial anxiety consumers in general, and consumers of alcohol in this case, are more sensitive to price increases, and are very likely to reduce consumption of more expensive alcoholic beverages, such as spirits and wine, or substitute with less expensive type of alcohol, namely beer. Come to think of it, it all makes perfect sense. In tough economic times, the use of alcohol is not so much for the enjoyment of the palate, but rather for the numbing of the senses. Thus, if financial anxiety is high and money is tight, many users of alcohol prefer to numb their senses with a less expensive type of alcohol.

Chapter Eight

Financial Anxiety and Risk-Based Decisions

Decision-making theories, or in short, decision theory, is an attempt to identify and classify specific rules governing our decision-making process. Most people face multiple decisions every day. Some are social decisions, some financial and some personal. The focus here is on a specific type of decisions many of us face daily; especially those who are in the field of business and finance—risk-based decisions. These are decisions in which the outcome carries a risk of financial loss, or chance of gain of money or other assets.

I noted earlier that the purpose of this section is to provide practical and useful information for readers who are engaged in business or financial decision-making with the hope that these new methods will make decision-making simpler, easier and more accurate. I completely intend to do that; but first I would like to provide a short theoretical background of decision science so readers can see how the thinking behind this fascinating field has evolved over the years to the current stage. I will point out flaws in the prevailing decision theories and propose a revised model for risk-based decision-making that incorporates the element of financial anxiety.

Risk-based decisions come in different forms. A simple risk-based decision, for example, is choosing to gamble when the odds for winning $100 are 30 percent. Some decisions are more complex—for example, choosing between a 70 percent probability of winning $100 and 40 percent chance of losing $200. As you can see, choices can get more and more risky and complex, which is why it was—and still is—so important to better understand the rules governing such decisions. The attempt to uncover the psychological and economical factors that play a role in risk-based decisions started a few hundred years ago and is still ongoing. In fact, this book (and this chapter in particular) is an enhancement of the current understanding of the governing rules of risk-based decisions and an improvement over the prevailing theories.

Utility Theory

The first and main attempt to explain choices made under risk was done by Daniel Bernoulli in 1738, when he initiated the framework for the expected utility theory titled "Exposition of a New Theory on the Measurement of Risk." The basic concept of expected utility theory is that the amount at risk, based on the given probability, is relative to the current wealth of the risk taker. In other words, a 30 percent probability of losing $1,000 carries a higher economic weight with an individual who has $100,000 in total wealth than with someone with a total wealth of $1,000,000. Therefore, according to the expected utility theory, a person with lesser means is more risk averse than a person with greater means. The same principle applies to gains—a gain of $1,000 carries higher economic weight to a person with lesser means than to someone with greater means.

Another important aspect of utility theory, introduced by Bernoulli in 1738, has to do with the distinction between the physical value of a gamble and the psychological impact of the same event. In other words, different amounts of money have varying level of psychological value, but the interval between the levels of money and the psychological value is not symmetrical. On this basis, Bernoulli developed a "conversion table" that shows the psychological value, or utility relative to various amounts of physical money. Below is an example of Bernoulli's utility table:

Wealth (millions)	1	2	3	4	5	6	7	8	9	10
Utility units	10	30	48	60	70	78	84	90	96	100

Here is a simple example of how Bernoulli's utility theory works. Let's assume that a person currently has $4 million in wealth. This person is faced with a choice of equal chances of gaining or losing $2 million. We know that the monetary impact of the gain or the loss is the same - $2 million, but would the psychological value be identical? Based on Bernoulli's utility theory, if this person gains the $2 million, this person will have a total of $6 million, and the added utility will be 18 utility points, which is the difference between $4 million at 60 utility points and $6 million at 78 utility points. If, however, the person loses the $2 million, the person's wealth will be reduced to $2 million, which means that this person's utility will decrease by 30 utility points—the difference between $4 million at 60 utility points, and $2 million at 30 utility points. On this basis, choosing to take the risk is not advisable.

Another aspect of Bernoulli's utility theory is somewhat obvious even in his era—people of greater financial means can take greater financial risks. If we look at the utility table above, it is clear that for a person with $10 in wealth, losing $1 million represents a psychological impact of 4 utility points, which is the difference between 96 and 100. On the other hand, a loss of $1 million by a person who has $2 million in wealth represents a psychological impact of 20 utility points, which is the difference between 30 and 10 utility points.

The Expected Utility Theory, or in short, utility theory, has been the prevailing theory in economics and decision science ever since; but more recently, the psychologists Kahneman and Tversky proposed a slightly different approach to risk-based decisions with the introduction of their highly acclaimed paper—"Prospect Theory: An Analysis of Decisions Under Risk." Prospect theory is based on the premise of utility theory that the expected utility of a loss or gain is relative to a reference point, as well as the differences between the physical and the psychological level of impact. However, prospect theory introduces a different reference point to the calculation of choice decisions.

Prospect Theory

The basic difference between utility theory and prospect theory, introduced by psychologists Kahneman and Tversky, is the additional reference point to the calculation of the utility of gain or loss. The additional reference point that prospect theory includes in the calculation is the difference in the wealth of the individual prior to the decision to take a chance on financial gain or loss. In other words, prospect theory asserts that that there is an additional factor impacting the decision of gain and loss, which is the change in wealth prior to the decision to take a chance or not. Thus, the reference point is the historical change in wealth and not the current state in wealth as proposed by utility theory.

Another important aspect of prospect theory is the distinction it makes between the psychological value of gains and losses. The difference in the psychological value between winning and losing, even if both are for the same amount, is an important addition to the science of risk-based decisions. Prospect theory introduced us to the asymmetry between the way people feel about losing and the way they feel about winning.

In one example Kahneman and Tversky ask: "Which do you choose; get $900 for sure, or a 90 percent chance to get $1,000", and conversely, "lose $900 for sure, or 90 percent chance to lose $1,000". If you are like most people, you would probably choose to take the $900 for sure in the first set of options, and to take your chances with the 90 percent loss in the second set of choices. Why? Because people hate to lose more than they love to win. Thus, the psychological impact of gaining or losing the same amount is not identical.

Consider this: by choosing to take the $900 for sure, your gain is guaranteed; and even though you had a slim chance of 10 percent to win the entire $1,000, you were risk averse and gave up on the chance of gaining an additional $100. On the other hand, in the second set of choices, you had two bad options—losing $900 for sure, or a 90 percent chance of losing $1,000. In this case, you have very little to lose by taking your chances with the 90 percent to lose $1,000 because the loss of $900 is guaranteed, and you have a slim chance of gaining $100. Hence, in cases where one is faced with two bad options or two losing propositions, one is more likely to be risk seeking and take a chance.

The difference in the psychological value between winning and losing is an important addition to the science of risk-based decisions. We now know that there is an asymmetry between the way people feel about losing and the way they feel about winning. In other words, for most people, losing $1,000 has a greater psychological value than winning $1,000. This distinction is very important; but it is also incomplete because, as we will see soon, it portrays only half the story. The second half of the story is that the asymmetry between winning and losing is not static. Rather, it is dynamic and it fluctuates with the level of financial anxiety.

The influence of financial anxiety on risk-based decisions is the central point in the concept of dynamic risk decisions I am introducing next. The idea is that our decision to take financial chances is impacted not only by the dollar amount in questions and the psychological value of the choices we face, but also by the level of financial anxiety at the time of the decision. As we will see next, our expectation of gain relative to the risk of loss varies based on our level of financial anxiety at the time of the decision making.

Money Anxiety Factor

Making choices that involve gain and loss is a way of life for any business or financial professional. For example, business people often have to make a decision on developing new products or services, and on investing in new equipment or vendors. Financial people, on the other hand, have to make decisions on investing in a new venture or founding a new project within existing companies. The common aspect of these types of decisions is that they carry risk because a new product or service may not succeed, and a new venture might not produce the desired financial results.

Often we don't even know the real odds of success or failure. By nature, new ventures of any kind don't have a track record, thus making it almost impossible to assess the chances of success or failure. Remember that the only method we know to try to project probability of success or failure is based on past experiences—we don't have a crystal ball. Moreover, keep in mind that even what we know from past experience might not be very relevant to future performance because circumstances can be different. And above all, we may even encounter a black swan event, an event that has not occurred in the past and is thus not part of our recorded experience. In such cases we don't even know what we don't know, as eloquently put by Nassim Nicholas Taleb, the author of "The Black Swan."

As you can see, gauging the odds of gain or loss in the world of business and finance is not simple, especially when it comes to endeavors that do not have historical track record. Therefore, unless we know differently, it is wise to establish the chances of gain and loss of such cases on equal footing, meaning an equal chance of winning or losing. On that basis, assuming that the chances for gain or loss are equal, the key question becomes: What is the level of financial gain that will offset the risk of loss?

We already know that for the most part people are risk averse; meaning that when faced with the choice of an equal chance of winning $100 and losing $100 most people will not take a chance. What if the amount of winning increases to $150, would this make a difference in the decision to take a chance? It depends. As we will see shortly, the amount we expect to gain, relative to the amount we may lose, is dynamic—based on our level of financial anxiety at the time of the decision making. Put simply, how much money will it take to convince us to take a chance relative to the amount we may lose considering our current level of financial anxiety? Next, I will answer this question and provide you with a very quick and simple way to calculate the specific dollar amount needed to gain in order to offset the risk of loss under varying levels of financial anxiety.

Studies of loss aversion found that the loss-aversion ratio ranges from 1.5 to 2.5 depending on the person's risk tolerance. In other words, when people are faced with equal chances of gaining or losing, they will expect the gain to be between 1.5 and 2.5 times the amount of the possible loss. The range of the risk-averse ratio varies based on the person's risk tolerance. Professional investors have greater risk tolerance because they spread the risk over a large range of options; thus they will be more likely to accept a gain of 1.5 times the amount of loss. Conversely, people who have lower risk tolerance are likely to have a risk aversion ratio of 2.5. For simplicity's sake, I will use the average risk-aversion ratio of 2.0, which is the acceptable ratio used in risk-based decisions models.

One point of clarification—the loss-aversion ratio is not without limits. This means that if you are a person of average financial means, using the average loss-aversion ratio of 2.0, you are likely to accept an equal chance of winning $200 or losing $100, but you are not likely to accept a chance of winning two million dollars or losing one million dollars—which may ruin you financially. So, of course, the amount of the risk is contingent upon the wealth and means of the person making the decision. Needless to say, the limits are different for large businesses and financial firms because they have greater means to absorb a loss.

Now let's see how we can arrive at the dollar amount of the gain that will be acceptable to offset a chance of loss in a dynamic environment of financial anxiety. The table below shows how to make gain and loss decisions within minutes, using a simple hand-held calculator. The first column on the left lists the three basic levels of consumer financial anxiety—high, average and low. The second column reflects the Money Anxiety Factor that we discussed in the previous chapter. As a reminder, the Money Anxiety Factor is the ratio of the current level of the Money Anxiety Index divided by the historical average of the Money Anxiety Index. The historical highest Money Anxiety Factor is about 2.0, and the lowest is about 0.5. The average, of course, is 1.0, which means that the current level of financial anxiety is the same as the historical average.

The next column is the average loss-aversion ratio of 2.0. If you are making a risk-based decision for someone who has a lower risk tolerance, you may substitute the loss-aversion ratio with 2.5; and for someone with higher risk tolerance, with 1.5. Finally, the last column on the right is the gain multiplier, which is a multiplication of the Money Anxiety Factor by the loss-aversion ratio. The gain multiplier is the number of times you need to multiply the amount at risk in order to arrive at an acceptable gain amount to offset the risk.

Money Anxiety Level	Money Anxiety Factor	Loss-Aversion Ratio (Average)	Gain Multiplier
High	2.0	2.0	4.0
Average	1.0	2.0	2.0
Low	0.5	2.0	1.0

Let's look at some examples. You are planning to invest $1,000 in a new endeavor with an equal chance of success or failure. What amount will you accept as a gain in order to take the chance of losing $1,000? If we are currently in a high level of financial anxiety, which we indeed are at the time of the writing of this chapter in late 2013, the Money Anxiety factor you should use is 2.0. Assuming that you have average tolerance to risk aversion, the risk-aversion ratio is also 2.0. Multiplying the Money Anxiety Factor by the loss-aversion ratio brings up the gain multiplier to 4.0. (2.0 times 2.0). Thus, you are likely to accept this chance only if the gain amount will be at least four times the $1,000 at risk, or $4,000.

If this calculation was done during times of average level of financial anxiety, with a Money Anxiety factor of 1.0, you would likely take this chance with an expected gain of $2,000, corresponding to a gain multiplier of 2.0 times the $1,000 at risk. And if you had to make the same decision during times of low level of financial anxiety, which has not occurred since the mid-1960s when the U.S. economy was booming, you would probably take your chances with gaining the same amount as you may lose—$1,000. Why? Because in extremely prosperous times, when money comes easily, people are more likely to be risk-seeking to the point of accepting a chance to gain just as much as they may lose.

Business and financial professionals can use this model to quickly and easily establish a level of accepted gain for different risk-based scenarios. The main point to remember here is that the accepted gain amount is not static, as proposed by prospect theory, but rather dynamic—based on the level of financial anxiety at the time of the risk-based decision. Moreover, this model can work inversely by establishing the dollar amount of the risk in accordance to the accepted gain by asking: How much do I want to gain from this endeavor, and then dividing this amount by the gain multiplier.

You can see now how the level of financial anxiety impacts not only our decisions regarding savings and spending as we discussed earlier in the book, but also our approach to risk-based decisions. This phenomenon is normal and natural for the same reasons we spend more during good economic times, and less during bad economic times. The difference is our inherent survival mechanism in the form of financial anxiety, which governs the way we react to savings, spending and financial risk-taking. But can financial anxiety spill over to other areas such as politics and elections? The answer is most definitely yes, as we will see in the next chapter.

Chapter Nine

Financial Anxiety and Politics

It's the Anxiety, Stupid

Do people really vote with their wallets and purses, as the saying goes? And if so, how do we know? After all, there is no specific question on the ballot asking people the reason they are voting for their candidate. One way to find out if there is a link between financial matters and election of candidates is to measure the level of financial anxiety prior to an election in order to see if there is a relation between the level of financial anxiety and the outcome of the election.

Not only is this concept logical, but it is also valid—as we will see shortly. There is, however, one stipulation—predicting how an election will turn out based on the level of financial anxiety requires that the candidate have a national track record. In other words, the Money Anxiety Index can predict the outcome of presidential re-elections because the incumbent candidate has a track record during the first term in office. The impact of an incumbent president on the economy during the first term will be reflected in the level of consumer financial anxiety during that time period. As a matter of fact, only the last year of the first term in office is needed to evaluate the president's probability of re-election.

During Bill Clinton's successful 1992 presidential campaign against the incumbent president George H. W. Bush, Clinton's campaign strategist James Carville coined the phrase: "It's the economy, stupid" which meant for the internal audience of Clinton's campaign workers that the economy should be one of the main messages on which to focus the campaign. Keep in mind that the year prior to the elections, in March 1991, 90 percent of polled Americans approved of President Bush's job performance after the successful military campaign in the first Iraq war. Therefore, any campaign message that would have focused on President Bush's handling of national security or international affairs would have not resonated well with voters. However, later the next year, which is the year that counts most for re-elections, Americans' opinions had turned sharply, and 64 percent of polled Americans disapproved of Bush's job performance in August 1992, mainly due to economic and financial matters.

George Carville's statement "It's the economy, stupid" is right—but only half right. The correct and more complete statement should have been "It's the anxiety, stupid" because, as you will see shortly, the level of consumer financial anxiety has been a major factor in the outcome of all nine presidential re-elections in the past 50 years. This is as far back as I could go with economic indicators, which means that in the last 50 years, the outcome of each presidential re-election was predictable by the Money Anxiety Index. Moreover, in the analysis I will present shortly, you will see that the predictability of presidential re-elections has no political affiliation. The Money Anxiety Index is "an equal opportunity index" because candidates of both political parties were equally impacted by the level of consumer financial anxiety at the time of the re-elections.

Anxiety and Presidential Re-elections

In January 2012, 11 months prior to the presidential election, I stated that Barack Obama, the incumbent president, would be re-elected to a second term if the Money Anxiety Index decreased below 89.2 by November 2012. Lo and behold, in November of 2012, when the presidential elections took place, the Money Anxiety Index stood at 86.2, and the incumbent president, Obama, was indeed re-elected to a second term.

This was not an isolated incident. The analysis below shows that in all presidential re-elections in the past 50 years, if the Money Anxiety Index decreased during the presidential election year, from January to November, the incumbent president was re-elected to a second term. If, however, the Money Anxiety Index increased between January and November of the election year, the incumbent president was not re-elected.

In addition to Obama's re-election, there were eight campaigns for second presidential terms in the last 50 years. Among these eight possible presidential re-elections, eight incumbent presidents lost, and five won re-election. All five incumbent presidents who won re-election were successful in lowering the Money Anxiety index between January and November of the election year. Prior to the 2012 election, President George W. Bush was re-elected when during his election year, from January to November 2004, the Money Anxiety Index decreased from 58.9 to 57.6—a decrease of 1.3 index points. Similarly, President William J. Clinton won a second term when during the election year, from January to November 1996, the Money Anxiety Index decreased from 69.2 to 68.8—a decrease of 0.4 index points.

Conversely, President James E. Carter was not re-elected to a second term. During the election year, from January to November 1980, the Money Anxiety Index increased from 80.3 to 98.4—an increase of 18.1 index points. Similarly, President George H.W. Bush was not re-elected to a second term. During the year of his campaign for re-election, from January to November 1992, the Money Anxiety Index increased from 81.7 to 85.7—an increase of 4.0 index points.

Historically, President Lyndon B. Johnson was elected after serving John F. Kennedy's remaining term. During Johnson's election year, from January to November 1964, the Money Anxiety Index decreased from 63.0 to 48.5—a decrease of 14.5 index points. The same was the case with the successful re-election of Richard M. Nixon. During his re-election year, from January to November 1972, the Money Anxiety Index decreased from 71.5 to 64.5—a decrease of 7.0 index points. Similarly, President Ronald W. Reagan won a second term. During his re-election year, from January to November 1984, the Money Anxiety Index decreased from 91.8 to 84.4—a decrease of 7.4 index points. On the other hand, during the election year of President Gerald R. Ford, who ran for re-election after serving the remaining term of President Nixon, from January to November 1976, the Money Anxiety Index increased from 90.2 to 93.2—an increase of 3.0 index points. He was defeated.

Clearly, the Money Anxiety Index is a reliable predictor of presidential re-elections. It shows that financial anxiety is a major factor in re-electing an incumbent president to a second term based on the relative level of financial anxiety consumers feel during the election year. There are two major implications for all those who are involved with campaign strategy for presidential elections. The first is that the year of the election, from January up to November, is the time period in which people evaluate the economic impact the incumbent president had on their financial standing; and second—it's the anxiety, stupid.

Anxiety is the Enemy of the Economy

Just as I was wrapping up the writing of this book, in October of 2012, the national event dominating the news was the partial government shutdown, which started on September 30, 2013, and ended on October 16. It's too soon to tell the extent of the impact this partial government shutdown will have on the level of consumer financial anxiety and the economy as a whole, but by looking at previous government shutdowns, we can have an idea of the impact it is likely to have on financial anxiety and the economy.

All together, there were 17 government shutdowns in the history of the U.S., excluding the current event of September and October of 2013. The last government shutdown occurred during the Clinton administration, nearly 18 years ago. That government shutdown was comprised of two shutdowns, one right after the other, with about one month between them; practically, two consecutive events. During these two consecutive shutdowns, the administration was lead by Democrats, with Bill Clinton as president, and both the Senate and the House of Representatives were controlled by Republicans. Let's take a look at the events of these two consecutive shutdowns, and how they impacted consumer financial anxiety.

The first shutdown of the Clinton Administration started on November 13, 1995 and lasted only five days. The underlying reason for that shutdown was that President Bill Clinton vetoed a continuing resolution passed by the Republican-controlled Congress. After a few days of government shutdown, a deal was reached allowing for 75-percent funding for four weeks, and Clinton agreed to a seven-year timetable for a balanced budget.

The second and lengthier government shutdown during the Clinton administration occurred a month later. On December 15, 1995, the Republicans demanded that President Clinton propose a budget with the seven-year timetable using Congressional Budget Office numbers, rather than Clinton's Office of Management and Budget numbers. Clinton refused. Eventually, after nearly 21 days of government shutdown, Congress and Clinton agreed to pass a compromise budget.

The good news is that these two consecutive government shutdowns did not have a long-lasting negative impact on consumer financial anxiety or the economy. The bad news is that these events did increase the level of consumer financial anxiety, and consequently consumer consumption. In October 1995, the month before the first Clinton-era government shutdown, the Money Anxiety Index stood at 65.6, a relatively low level of consumer financial anxiety. During most of that year, consumer financial anxiety was declining—a sign of economic growth.

By November 1995, the month when the first Clinton-era shutdown occurred, the level of consumer financial anxiety increased to 67.1—an increase of 1.5 index points in one month. In December 1995, which is when the second consecutive Clinton-era government shutdown occurred, the Money Anxiety Index increased again to 67.4, and in January 1996, which is when this particular government shutdown ended, consumer financial anxiety increased again to 68.3. All together, the level of consumer financial anxiety during the Clinton administration shutdown increased by 2.7 index points.

Clearly, the economic uncertainty associated with government shutdowns increased the level of consumer financial anxiety. There are those who are directly impacted by the shutdown, such as some government employees, and some suppliers and contractors of governmental agencies. Moreover, businesses that provide services to government employees, such as restaurants, dry cleaning and the like, are impacted directly from reduced business activity. But the ripple effect of a government shutdown goes much beyond those who are impacted directly. The indirect impact of a government shutdown is the increased level of consumer financial anxiety shared by most people, which is felt in the level of consumer spending.

A look at the level of consumer spending during the two consecutive shutdowns in November 1995, December 1995 and January 1996, shows that consumer spending decreased by $11 billion in January of 1996, while the shutdown was still in effect for the first week of the January. In case you are wondering if a decrease in consumer spending during January, right after the holiday season, is "normal"—it is not. The year before, in January 1995, consumer spending increased by $8 billion and the year after, in January 1997, consumer spending increased by $34 billion after the holiday season. Is it likely that the financial anxiety over the prolonged government shutdown is the reason consumers halted their spending in January of 1996—yes, very likely.

There is another message here for the executive and legislative branches of the government, regardless of political affiliation. The longer the economic uncertainty lasts, the higher the level of consumer financial anxiety, and the greater the negative impact on the economy. In other words, anxiety is the enemy of the economy, and a large-scale event that increases the level of consumer financial anxiety will have an adverse effect on the economy.

We live in an era of connectivity and dependency, where some events can have a ripple effect on the lives of most people. We are all connected through a maze of economic activities where one person's spending is another person's earning. Collectively, as consumers, we fuel about 70 percent of the U.S. economy. Thus, if a large enough group of consumers, due to increased level of financial anxiety, halts or slows down their consumption, we are all affected.

Throughout this book, you have seen the link between our physiology, psychology and our behavioralogy. This trilogy of mankind should be the mantra of every politician, lawmaker and any other people who impact large-scale events, because their decisions and actions will have financial and economic implications for all of us. We no longer live in a compartmental society, where an event in one segment is irrelevant to other groups—we are all in this together.

I leave you with this thought in mind: no matter how advanced we are going to be in technology and science, our basic human nature is forever. Therefore, whether you are involved in business, finance or politics, always keep in mind that uncertainty breeds anxiety and anxiety is the enemy of the economy.

Resources

The following list provides additional information and links to resources such as the Money Anxiety Index, the Money Anxiety Factor and the Money Anxiety Historical data.

Money Anxiety Index

The Money Anxiety current month's index is calculated and published on the first week of every calendar month. The index is available to the public at www.moneyanxietyindex.com

Money Anxiety Factor

The Money Anxiety Factor, which is the ratio of the current month's index divided by the historical average of the index, is also available on the Money Anxiety Index website. The Money Anxiety Factor can be used to calculate the real price elasticity of demand for products and services, as well as the real amount of money required to offset risk-based decisions.

Money Anxiety Historical Data

A monthly time series showing the Money Anxiety Index for the past 50 years is available for licensing. The historical data ranges from January of 1959 to the current month. The Money Anxiety Historical Data is helpful in identifying statistical relations between the level of consumer financial anxiety and demand for various products and services. Additionally, the Money Anxiety Historical Data can be used to determine trends in the state of the economy. To inquire about licensing and using the Money Anxiety Historical Data, please contact drgeller@moneyanxiety.com

About the Author

Dr. Dan Geller is an experienced researcher and analyst, and an expert in statistical modeling. He developed the Money Anxiety concept and index after observing how a combination of economic indicators and factors impacts consumers' financial behavior. Specifically, he observed how financial anxiety impacts the saving and spending patterns of consumers, and the impact such changes in financial behavior have on the economy.

Based on these observations, Dr. Geller developed a new segmentation method called Behavioralogy, which defines the financial behavior of consumers during various levels of financial anxiety. Behavioralogy identified six types of financial orientation: Mattress Money, Durable Diet, Power Play, Tiny Treats, Rate Race and Castle Craze.

Dr. Geller is frequently featured in national and financial publications, such as The Wall Street Journal, The New York Times, Bloomberg/Newsweek, and has appeared on CNBC, Fox News Radio, and numerous regional programs. Dr. Geller earned his Ph.D. in Business Administration from Touro University, and has published numerous peer-reviewed studies in professional publications. He resides in San Rafael, California.

CPSIA information can be obtained at www.ICGtesting.com
Printed in the USA
BVOW11s2046280116

434293BV00013B/83/P